D0866794

REIGN OF TERROR

REIGN OF TERROR

The Budapest Memoirs of
Valdemar Langlet 1944-1945

Valdemar Langlet
Foreword by Monika Langlet and Pieter Langlet
Introduction by Sune Persson
Translation by Graham Long

Frontline Books, London/Skyhorse Publishing, New York

Reign of Terror: The Budapest Memoirs of Valdemar Langlet 1944-1945
This edition published in 2012 by Frontline Books,
an imprint of Pen & Sword Books Ltd,
47 Church Street, Barnsley, S. Yorkshire, S70 2AS
www.frontline-books.com
and
Published and distributed in the United States of America and Canada
by Skyhorse Publishing, 307 West 36th Street, 11th Floor, New York, NY 10018
www.skyhorsepublishing.com
Skyhorse Publishing books may be purchased in bulk at special discounts
for sales promotion, corporate gifts, fund raising, or educational purposes.
Special editions can also be created to specifications.
For details, contact Special Sales Department, Skyhorse Publishing,
307 West 36th Street, 11th Floor, New York, NY 10018 or email
info@skyhorsepublishing.com

Copyright © Valdemar Langlet, 2012
Foreword copyright © Monika and Pieter Langlet, 2012
Introduction copyright © Sune Persson, 2012
Translation © Frontline Books/Pen & Sword Books Limited, 2012
All photographs copyright © Miklós Gulyás

The right of Valdemar Langlet to be identified as the author of this work has been
asserted by him in accordance with the Copyright, Designs and Patents Act 1988.

Frontline edition: ISBN 978-1-84832-659-0
Skyhorse edition: ISBN 978-1-62087-809-5

Publishing history
First published as Verk och Dagar i Budapest by
Wahlström & Widstrand, Stockholm, in 1946.

The Publisher would express his gratitude to Thanks To Scandinavia for their
contribution to the production of this first English-language edition.
This book would not have been possible without their generous support.

All rights reserved. No part of this publication may be reproduced, stored in or
introduced into a retrieval system, or transmitted, in any form, or by any means
(electronic, mechanical, photocopying, recording or otherwise) without the prior written
permission of the publisher. Any person who does any unauthorized act in relation to this
publication may be liable to criminal prosecution and civil claims for damages.

CIP data records for this title are available from the British Library

Library of Congress Cataloging-in-Publication Data is available on file.

For more information on our books, please visit
www.frontline-books.com, email info@frontline-books.com
or write to us at the above address.

Printed and bound in the UK by the MPG Books Group

Typeset by M.A.T.S. Typesetters, Leigh-on-Sea, Essex

CONTENTS

LIST OF ILLUSTRATIONS

(between pages 78 and 79)

1. Valdemar Langlet, chief delegate in Hungary for the Swedish Red Cross (1944–5).
2. A Swedish Red Cross 'letter of protection'.
3. A page from a 'letter of protection', with Valdemar Langlet's signature.
4. A Red Cross plaque, with text in Swedish and Hungarian.
5. Elisabeth Bridge, spanning the Danube, was blown up by the Germans.
6. Kálvin Square in central Budapest at the end of the war.
7. Valdemar Langlet at the gates of the Swedish Embassy in Budapest.
8. Monsignore Gennaro Verolino, the Papal Nuncio's secretary.
9. Soviet soldiers crossing the Danube and approaching Budapest in December 1944.
10. Inhabitants of Budapest scavenging meat from the corpses of horses.
11. Trams, cars and pedestrians were plunged into the icy waters of the Danube when the Margaret Bridge was demolished by accident.
12. A street in Budapest named after Langlet.
13. A ceremony at a school named after Langlet.

FOREWORD

Stockholm, Sweden
November 2011

Dear Grandpa,

Do you remember when you walked straight over the gravel we had just raked down together with you? Your big boots left some huge footprints in the wavy patterns we had made with our rakes. The two of us, brother and sister, were trying to keep our balance on the edge so as not to disturb the freshly raked gravel! Your deep and kindly baritone voice consoled us by explaining that we'd raked the gravel because it was Saturday and the end of the week and we'd finished off the week's work. You said it was just something called a ritual, giving a sense of security and marking the passage of time.

It was summer time at the end of the 1940s, and we were spending those sunny summer days in the garden with you. It's over sixty years ago. We were staying at our house next to yours and grandma's. You were a bit over seventy-five years of age and we were a mere four and five. At that time we didn't understand much of what we did together with you or everything you used to tell us.

You used to talk a lot about photosynthesis, the ecological balance in Mother Nature, and you said that every plant is equal in value. Saying this, you carefully pulled out a few weeds and let them dry out in the sun while we went on weeding the flower

vii

beds. Didn't make sense, was what we thought. And nowadays, ourselves growing and cultivating using ecological methods, we understand that weeds have to dry out before landing on the compost heap to become once again usable soil material.

It was also amusing (but at the same time rather touching) when you would sit on a stool from the kitchen working in the garden while we two would squat down beside you. Now that we are both getting on for seventy, we realise too well why you spared your knees by sitting on the stool.

We would study the bees buzzing in the foxgloves in front of the smithy. You got the snapdragons to bite our fingertips and it didn't even hurt! Flowers don't need to be nice and colourful and visible, you used to tell us; and you showed us the tiny yellow-green flowers on the creeper which tangled its way around the little garden cottage with its large, heart-shaped leaves. You explained to us why roses need their thorns when they scratch us, and why the wasp stung Monika in the neck when it found itself being trapped. In the orchard we were fascinated when you stretched up to reach the apples on the top branches using that long pole with the basket at the end.

It was exciting going down into your dark, chilly cellar with that mixture of mouldy air and fresh apple smell. The shelves were full of glass jars, and we could see their contents of fruit, vegetables and eggs. The bottles of juice stood neatly in line, duly labelled. The earthenware jars contained lingonberry jam and pickled mushrooms. The apples, nicely wrapped in sheets of newspaper, were stacked layer upon layer in crates. The lovely red apples were to be saved up for Christmas and given a shine over before they landed among the Christmas fare.

You told us about foreign places and the hardships you'd had to endure. How you and your brother Alex had discovered the world on horseback. We didn't understand it all, for sure, but it was all very thrilling, in any case; for instance, how you operated on a Mongolian chieftain in his Mongol tent called a yurt, and how it was made perfectly plain for you that if the chieftain died, so would you too. As we got older you would be telling us more about your extensive and adventurous travels.

You had a lot of friends around the world, and friends are a richer source of wealth than money – that was always your philosophy. You told us of how through courtesy and a humble attitude you had always managed to acquire food and lodging during your trips. Find out how you say 'Porridge' and 'Good day!' in the countries you come to, was your advice to us, and you'll always get by. Thank you, grandpa, we have successfully followed your advice, though Monika must admit that she's never really liked porridge all that much so she used bread instead, but the courtesy part we've both always tried to embrace, and not only on our travels, by the way.

You used to use expressions and proverbs whenever we had a chat together. For example, every time a little bird appeared and perched near us you would repeat 'Keep still, little birdie, I'm not going to hurt you, I'm just going to pour a little salt on your tail, that's all!', whereupon with your finger and thumb you made as if to actually pour salt on its tail. At the time we didn't of course understand what you meant by this, but we thought it was funny and we would say the same whenever we saw a bird, especially if it was a wagtail. As we got older you were able to tell us the expression has been around for hundreds of years in many other countries, and that it worked as a spell to capture birds – if you got so close to a bird that you could pour salt on its tail, then your chances were good of being able to catch it.

You were a man of rather few words and a quiet disposition – it was mostly grandma who did the talking – but you loved playing with words, and your eyes lit up behind those heavy glasses of yours whenever you cracked a joke or punned. In the course of the years, anyway, you came to talk with us about much more than gardens, plants and your travels. You would talk about anything from Mark Twain, Tolstoy, Spinoza and the American Civil War to the thinking behind Esperanto. Though we were much older then, we probably understood and remember today only a part of what you told us.

You often wore a white Cossack shirt and high riding boots, well worn in, and could move with a natural dignity which made it difficult to imagine you running. You also gave us the impression of a tactful discretion as you spoke to us or sat and read with your glasses high up on your forehead, which didn't make it easy to picture you as an active hero. We don't remember you ever running, but much later, when we were considerably much older, we realised that you were a hero – a true hero.

Your grandchildren,
Monika and Pieter Langlet

INTRODUCTION

R AOUL WALLENBERG is probably one of the most famous Swedes in the world in recent times. He was the second man – after Sir Winston Churchill – to be awarded honorary US citizenship. The US Holocaust Memorial Museum is located at Raoul Wallenberg Place SW, in Washington, DC. In the hagiography surrounding the figure of Wallenberg, he is presented as the man who in the last months of the Second World War in Budapest acted courageously to save the lives of tens of thousands of Jews from the Germans and Hungarians who at that time were murdering innocent people *en masse* in the city. Although all the accolades heaped on Wallenberg were – and are – entirely well-deserved, one wonders, however, why other brave men and women who saved the lives of hundreds or thousands of people during those harrowing months in Budapest seem to have been forgotten by history, even in their home countries. One of those forgotten heroes is another Swede, Valdemar Langlet.

Valdemar Langlet was born on 17 December 1872, in Lerbo, a small community south of Stockholm. His father was a well-known architect, who designed the Norwegian parliament building in Oslo, among other buildings. His mother was the author of a large number of books for children and young people, as well as a founding member of the Swedish journal *Idun*. Young Valdemar took his academic degree in Humanities at the University of Uppsala, and later received scholarships which took him for further studies to Germany, Austria and

Switzerland. He was gifted at foreign languages. At an early age he took an interest in the new artificial language Esperanto, and founded an Esperanto club in Uppsala, the first in Sweden and the second one in the world.

Langlet was, however, an adventurous man, fond of horse-riding. Following his university examination he set out on a long journey through Russia, Eastern Europe and Asia Minor. This resulted in his first book, *Till häst genom Ryssland* ('On Horseback Across Russia').[1] After mastering the Russian language, Langlet worked as a journalist from 1909 to 1924, in charge of the editorial section of one of Sweden's leading morning newspapers, *Svenska Dagbladet*, a conservative Stockholm paper. He was active in the Swedish support for Finland's independence from Russia, and as a result in 1918 was awarded Finland's *Frihetskors* ('Freedom Cross').

In 1899 Langlet married Signe Blomberg, and the couple made a honeymoon trip to Russia, Siberia and Samarkand. The journey was given financial assistance by Oscar II, King of Sweden and Norway, providing the couple with a train compartment of their own all the way from St. Petersburg. Following the death of Langlet's wife in 1921, he visited the Soviet Union in 1923, being the first conservative Swedish journalist to do so. During his visit he met Nina Borovko, who became his second wife in 1925. Nina was a pianist, and she moved to Sweden to complete her musical studies. Langlet was then fifty-two years old, and Nina only twenty-nine. The difference in their ages – twenty-three years – did not prevent their marriage from lasting the remaining thirty-five years of Valdemar's life. After living in Dubrovnik for a few years, they moved to Budapest in 1931. Valdemar celebrated their move to the new country by crossing the whole of Hungary on horseback, at the age of sixty! This journey was documented in another book, *Till häst genom Ungern* ('On Horseback Across Hungary').[2]

The Langlets stayed in the Hungarian capital until the horrifying final days of the Second World War. Langlet learnt the difficult language of the Magyars, and worked in Budapest as a university lecturer teaching Swedish. Thanks to his proficiency in Hungarian, in 1938 he was attached to the Swedish Legation in Budapest as an unpaid cultural attaché. The Langlets built up a large network of friends, particularly within the cultural establishment but also among the upper echelons of Budapest society. He gradually achieved a thorough knowledge of the ins and outs of Hungarian society, and noticed the strong anti-Semitic currents rife in it. There are stories of how he himself had to protect his Jewish students from attacks from their Christian fellows.

From 1941 on Hungary had been fighting against the Soviet Union as an ally of Nazi Germany. The Hungarians refused, however, to deport their approximately 800,000 Jews. In 1944 Germany occupied Hungary and, in tandem with the Hungarian authorities, now rounded up opponents to the war. The Nazi *Endlösung*, the liquidation of the Hungarian Jews, also began, mainly in the countryside. The Hungarian Regent, Admiral Horthy, stopped the deportations on 6 July 1944 following strong international pressure, including a very harsh letter from the King of Sweden, Gustav V. When on 15 October 1944 Horthy announced an armistice with the Soviet Union he was arrested by the Germans, who declared a continuation of the war and installed the Hungarian Fascist party, the *Nyilas*, the Arrow Cross, as the new Hungarian government. The deportations and massacres of the Jews, now in Budapest itself, was renewed with the hoodlums from the Arrow Cross as willing executioners.

In 1944, at the age of seventy-two, Valdemar Langlet, helped by his Nina, came face to face with History. Now started their frantic work to save all kinds of persecuted Hungarians in their worst hours and days and months of torment. As Árpád Rátkai wrote:

The Langlets' Lónyai Street residence was packed to the rafters with refugees. As Esperantists, they accepted everyone, regardless of language, nationality, religion and citizenship. By April 1944 they had accepted so many escapees who were lying low in their residence that, in the strict meaning of the word, there was no room for Valdemar, who had to sleep at a friend's house.[8]

It was now, some time in May 1944, that Langlet started producing his famous 'letters of protection', or *Schutzbriefe*. These letters contained texts in Swedish, Hungarian and German. They constituted a kind of identity card, imitating normal passports with a photograph, personal data and a Swedish Red Cross (SRK) stamp. They were signed 'Langlet Valdemar *delegierter*', although at that time he was not formally a delegate of the Red Cross. These 'letters of protection' were issued without the knowledge of the SRK or of the Swedish Legation in Budapest. It was not until 17 August that Langlet finally received his official designation as an 'SRK delegate at the Swedish Legation in Hungary'. His unilateral and arbitrary use of the SRK logo and its prestige led to considerable criticism and rancour within the SRK leadership in Stockholm. The people at the top, with the eighty-year-old Prince Carl as President and Count Folke Bernadotte as Vice-President, obviously never understood the severity of the situation in Budapest, the chaos all around, and the enormous pressure being put on the heroic figures helping out throughout the city.

The consequences, in any case, were to be severe. SRK in Stockholm, and to some extent the Legation in Budapest as well, never really trusted Langlet. His odd official position, as a Red Cross delegate subordinated to the Swedish Legation, obviously was designed to rein him in. SRK also twice tried to persuade the Legation to dismiss him, and Langlet did in fact offer his resignation. In both cases, however, the Swedish minister, Danielsson, refused to dismiss Langlet, whose enormous efforts and achievements were deeply appreciated by Danielsson, himself a somewhat unconventional Swedish diplomat.

Nonetheless, Valdemar Langlet never received a single penny – or rather *pengö* – from the Swedish Red Cross. Nor did he receive any salary or the SRK uniform he had requested. The enormous rescue apparatus he had built up in Budapest was wholly financed by his own money and by donations from Hungarians, most of whom were Jews. A whole range of apartments, entire houses, castles, countryside estates and convents were placed at the disposal of Langlet and his Red Cross – all at no cost to the Swedish Red Cross!

We do not know who invented the famous 'letters of protection'. It might have been Langlet himself, or his colleague at the Swedish Legation, Secretary Per Anger, or the Swiss Vice-Consul Carl Lutz, or the Secretary-General of the SRK in Hungary, Alexander Kasser (as told to Runberg, Langlet's biographer, in 1999 by Kasser's wife).[7] Whatever the case, they were issued from May 1944, long before Wallenberg arrived in Budapest on 9 July. Nor do we know how many 'letters of protection' were actually issued. Runberg quotes estimates ranging from 2,000 (as officially approved by the Hungarian government) up to 25,000 (Nina Langlet and the Mosaic Congregation in Budapest). Almost all the material was destroyed during the horrific battle waged between the Germans and the Soviets in Budapest, often in house-to-house fighting, in late 1944.

It should also be pointed out that these 'letters of protection' had no real legal status at all. As Langlet himself made clear, 'they were nothing but a bluff!' On many occasions, however, they did indeed work! The uneducated German and Arrow Cross soldiers, having no idea of national or international law, often accepted these documents. In Levine's book (p. 142)[6] an interesting cartoon from a Hungarian newspaper (*Pesti Posta*, 10 September 1944) depicts a Hungarian policeman asking a heavily-stereotyped Jew: 'Why are you not wearing your Yellow Star?' whereupon the Jew replies: 'Has not the Commissar ever seen a Swedish citizen?'

These now-famous 'letters of protection' served the Langlets in building up a large SRK organisation which in the end consisted of sixteen different divisions, among them twelve Hungarian hospitals, fourteen homes for the elderly, 'sheltered' houses within the so-called International Ghetto with room for more than 3,000 refugees, forty-seven homes for children (most of them under the supervision of another SRK delegate, Ms Asta Nilsson), seven convents and two monasteries (in cooperation with the Papal Nuncio). This huge apparatus was administered by scores of volunteers, most of them Jews, working entirely without pay. On 11 December 1944, however, Langlet was forced to stop all these activities after a series of threats and a final ultimatum from the Arrow Cross regime. On Christmas Eve Arrow Cross militiamen raided the Swedish Legation. Valdemar, sentenced to death by the Arrow Cross, had to go underground together with Nina. He was now quite weak and in bad health.

By mid-January 1945 the Soviet army had liberated the whole of Pest, the eastern part of the city where both Langlet and Wallenberg lived, and the Langlets together with the Swedish Legation were put under Soviet protection. On 17 January Wallenberg left Pest to see – as he believed – the Soviet Marshal Malinovsky, but was never seen again outside the Soviet Union. Langlet, however, was unstoppable. On 2 February he received permission from the Soviet commander in Pest to restart his Red Cross activities. So he did, until the Swedish Legation was compelled to leave Budapest on 15 March. Langlet, sick and bed-ridden, had to stay. The Swedish Red Cross now ordered Langlet to close down the SRK's activities since, in the absence of a diplomatic presence, they were no longer permitted. Langlet, however, once more out-manoeuvred SRK headquarters in Stockholm. A few days before SRK operations were dismantled, Langlet had founded a Swedish–Hungarian Society to which the whole organisation was handed over: personnel, premises, all the resources and the entire network of contacts. Thus the range of activities built up over the years by Langlet and his wife was able to continue and the SRK had no say in the matter.

Nina and Valdemar Langlet left Hungary on 26 May 1945. Valdemar's health had deteriorated to such an extent that he had to be carried. He would never more see his beloved

Budapest. After a long and tiresome journey, by ship from Istanbul, the Langlets finally set foot on Swedish soil in Göteborg on 2 September. They were now totally destitute, but would never receive any form of help or remuneration either from the Swedish Red Cross or from the Swedish government. They settled in a small cottage in Lerbo, close to Valdemar's childhood home, but moved to Stockholm in 1955. Valdemar made a meagre living writing articles for newspapers, while Nina gave piano lessons. Valdemar Langlet died on 16 October 1960, by which time he was largely a forgotten man in Sweden. His wife Nina was to survive him by twenty-eight years, until 1988.

Valdemar Langlet was awarded the Swedish Red Cross Medal in silver in 1946 and became a Knight of the Swedish North Star (*Nordstjärneorden*) in 1949. Since then he has received no attention at all from Swedish authorities, and not even from the Swedish Red Cross. On the other hand, in 1965 he was recognised, together with his wife Nina, by the Israeli Yad Vashem Holocaust memorial as one of the Righteous Gentiles.

The vivid memory of the Langlets and their heroic work in 1944–5 has, however, been kept alive in Hungary. In 1945 Valdemar was awarded the Hungarian Republic's Order of the Cross. Nowadays, in the centre of Budapest, Valdemar has his own street, *Lánglet Valdemár útca*, his own public school, *Lánglet Valdemár áltános iskola*, and a plaque commemorating him set up by the Budapest City Council in 1986. In addition, in the summer of 2010, the same city council renamed the River Danube's quays in the centre of the city after those who had rescued people from being shot there during the Arrow Cross period. One quay is now named Raoul Wallenberg, and another after Nina and Valdemar Langlet: *Valdemár és Nina Lánglet rákpart*.

Langlet books
1. Valdemar Langlet, *Till häst genom Ryssland* (Stockholm: 1898).

2. Valdemar Langlet, *Till häst genom Ungern* (Stockholm: 1934).
3. Valdemar Langlet, *Verk och dagar i Budapest* (Stockholm: 1946).
4. Nina Langlet, *Kaos i Budapest. Berättelsen om hur svensken Valdemar Langlet räddade tiotusentals människor undan nazisterna i Ungern.* (Vällingby: 1982). *The Swedish Rescue Operation* (Budapest: 1988).

Secondary sources
5. Paul A. Levine, *From Indifference to Activism. Swedish Diplomacy and the Holocaust, 1938-1944* (Diss. 2nd ed. Uppsala: 1998).
6. Paul A. Levine, *Raoul Wallenberg in Budapest. Myth, History and Holocaust* (London and Portland OR: 2010).
7. Björn Runberg, *Valdemar Langlet. Räddare i faran* (Bromma, 2000). *The Forgotten Hero. Valdemar Langlet* (Budapest: 2007).
8. Árpád Rátkai, *Valdemar Langlet and the 'Grateful' Budapest* (Szeged: 2010. English version by Andrea Hegyesi, Australia, revised by David R. Curtis, Great Britain).
9. www.sv.wikipedia.org/Valdemar Langlet
10. www.hu.wikipedia.org/valdemar_langlet

Sune Persson
Göteborg, Sweden, 2012

PRELUDE

JUST fifty years ago two students from Uppsala set out on a
long trip, each with 200 Swedish crowns in their pockets.
In 1895 that was still money to speak of. Not much for a
journey through half of Europe, admittedly, but still
sufficient for a two-month test of endurance.

Cycling the length and breadth of southern Finland was
already something of an achievement for a 22-year-old who
hadn't seen so very much of the world outside his own back-
yard. And then came Russia: the brilliant Imperial city on the
banks of the Neva, the wonderful Moscow of the old Tsars, and
a first visit to the great prophet, Lev Tolstoy; a three-day
journey down to the Black Sea followed by a three-week hike
through the Jaila mountains above the enchantingly lovely
Russian riviera, with the now famous Yalta as our point of
departure and arrival. After which we enjoyed a sunny day and
a moonlit night on the Black Sea to reach Abdul Hamid's
Constantinople to stay a week, an amazing dream which
seemed to defy reality . . .

And then an abrupt turn northwards and homeward bound
via the Danube estuary, Bucharest, Sinaia and Budapest, where
they were preparing an exhibition the following year to
celebrate the Hungarian kingdom's thousand years of
existence. The city was in a ferment, bustling with activity,
huge suspension bridges over the wide river under construction, as well as an enormous neo-Gothic parliament
building, and an impressive array of churches and museums.

This was a recently-awakened royal nation, eager to indulge in architectural orgies in art nouveau style, bent solely upon 'asserting itself' within the Hapsburg empire as the larger party in a union which had been formed a long time back – we ourselves on the Scandinavian peninsula had of course our own set of problems of a similar nature.

That was Budapest in 1895 – what an experience for a young student whose scanty travelling funds were barely sufficient to cover the ticket home and lightning visits to Vienna, Prague, Dresden and Berlin, and who therefore was obliged to bid a quick farewell to the Queen of the Danube! He made a promise – there and then, and in spite of his travelling companion's bitter scepticism – to return the following summer to take a closer look at this romantic nation, which was already in the process of digging up the capital's streets to make way for an underground railway system connecting with the City Park, where one exhibition after another was being erected.

'You're nuts,' said my friend. 'You'll never come here again! If it hadn't been for me, you'd still be loitering around the Sinaia mountain range. Remember how I grabbed hold of you and got you into the train compartment so you wouldn't remain down there, all bound up in your infatuation for all the beautiful and interesting features of that area, where you'd probably have died of hunger, penniless! Come on now, you surely realise that you first have to get down and study in your student flat back home in Uppsala for the next couple of years'.

Yet it did turn out the way I wanted. The following year I was itching to travel again. A few articles I had written in the local press provided enough funds for a fresh excursion in an easterly and southerly direction. I witnessed an incredibly pompous Imperial coronation in Moscow together with a different but equally crazy Uppsala student, followed by some unforgettable days spent at Tolstoy's home in Yasnaya Poliana; a swift trip to Cossack country on the river Don; a 1,000km river trip on the Volga from Tsaritsyn to the exclusively Russian exhibition at Nizhni Novgorod – cities which now go under the names of Stalingrad and

Gorki while their former nomenclature is now only available in encyclopaedias.

By a stroke of luck – there on the bridge over the Volga – I found myself in the company of an artist who had recently daubed a picture for the exhibition: a panorama of the oil metropolis Baku, although he hadn't even been there! It wasn't difficult to get this old daredevil to join me on a 6,000km trip through Poland, Hungary, Bosnia and Italy. After a couple of remarkable weeks in the repressed Poland and its two old capital cities, Warsaw and Cracow, together with a quick visit to the salt mines at Wieliczka and their underground lake, we made a bold climb over the 2,000m-high Tatra mountain range to avoid the train journey around the Carpathians, and soon I found myself for a second time in Budapest – in spite of my friend's prophecy to the contrary!

Budapest's anniversary exhibition was ready, and scintillatingly attractive. The 'Queen of the Danube', as she was fondly known, fully lived up to her name, and I experienced what many of my compatriots later experienced: whoever has set eyes on this city once, that person longs to go back there, sooner or later. After a few years, we were there again, the painter and myself: travelling to the extensive *puszta* by Hortobágy, that vast green ocean of plains with its very own Vesuvius – the distant blue Tokay mountain on the horizon towards the north. The place abounded with young horses in their thousands; hunters, dogs, hares and wild geese. You could see white oxen with horns shaped like old-fashioned lyres, uniformed *panduri* on horseback (the gendarmes of that era), and shepherds dressed in ankle-length, rounded woollen sheepskins or magnificently-embroidered matted capes. You could enjoy dancing with lovely young girls – their cheeks round and rosy, their eyes black or pepper-brown – clad in the national costumes of white, red and green; all under the clear blue October sky with air as fresh and invigorating as the slightly acidic local wine.

The years went by, and we all had to go through something we had never dreamed would happen: the First World War, with what we considered to be the unthinkable destruction of the greatest cultural and material values. The Hungarian people had in no way wished to be part of this 'witches' brew', and had nothing to gain from the issues at stake, magnified into an enormous conflict and brought about by criminal so-called 'statesmen'. And yet they were drawn into the unhappy conflict, and in the final outcome suffered perhaps more than any other participant: it cost them the loss of two-thirds of their territory and population. They paid the price of others' crimes as fanatical, short-sighted and ignorant diplomats sat around a green table (in the words of that rather sad figure, Arthur Balfour) and dealt out parcels of land they had never seen to people they knew nothing about ...

For my part, I had spent almost a quarter of a century sitting rather still at an editorial desk or in some social meeting, and I was the father of a couple of grown-up boys, themselves students, who had already started out in life, when once again my youthful urge to travel took hold of me. What would the defeated Germany look like these days, the Germany whose years of splendour I had beautiful memories of from my shorter trips there, and from a longer stay studying at Heidelberg University? Or the Russia of the former Tsars, the Russia I'd crossed back and forth several times – 1,500km with Cossacks on one occasion – and which was now the communist-led Soviet Union? What sort of countenance could Poland now offer up, finally forging a national life of its own, after those years of yearning for freedom and independence through the 1890s, something which had left such an indelible impression on this visiting Swede? And what was life like nowadays in the little of Hungary that remained after the Treaty of Trianon, part of the famous 'King Stephen's territories', whose splendid development around the turn of the century I had witnessed?

Berlin and Vienna, Warsaw and Moscow, in 1923 – that's another story, valid in this context inasmuch as a contrast to the conditions prevailing in Budapest and the Hungarian kingdom which had been carved up so cruelly. There I met a people who, confronted by their unhappiness, gritted their teeth and stubbornly put their faith in a future in which the motto, heard everywhere, proclaimed that *'Nem, nem, soha'* . . . 'No, no, never' . . . shall we accept this hideous carving-up of our beloved land! Within a short period of time, however, the situation within the country had stabilised, and following a brief period of confusion the ancient kingdom's constitution had been re-instated. As Regent and pretender to the throne stood a naval man of prime quality at the helm: Admiral Nikolaus Horthy (*nagybányai Horthy Miklós* in Hungarian). At his side, for a full decade to come, he had the assistance of the country's foremost statesman, not to say its *only* great statesman in the present generation, Count István Bethlen, a descendant of Gábor Bethlen, a contemporary of the Swedish King Gustav II Adolf and his brother-in-law, the Prince of Siebenbürgen.

At the time of my fourth visit to the country, Hungary's inflation rate was so low that an abundant dinner at any of the principal restaurants of the capital cost little more than a miserable loaf of bread in Vienna, while in Moscow for a newspaper or a tram ride you had to spend a million roubles, and one *Reichsmark* in Berlin gradually sank to one billionth of its original value! Later Bethlen managed to stabilise the value of a new currency called the *pengö* (literally 'clinking') which replaced the devalued *korona* (the Austrian 'crown'). This new currency survived quite well right into the Second World War until its collapse in the two Nazi upheavals of March and October 1944.

The difficulties Hungary had to contend with during the two decades of relative peace, however, were quite considerable. A dearth of capital required measures involving requests for foreign loans; from our country, Sweden, too, the large so-called 'match' loan in exchange for a monopoly of business. These loans could barely yield interest in a state where the means of production had lost both organisation and coherence through the violent dismemberment of the country and the setting up of new customs posts. The latter unfortunately broke up the previous excellent economic union made up by the old Danubian monarchy, of which it had once been said that 'if it didn't exist, it would have to be invented'. Hungary was now suffering from having too large a workforce. Plans and calculations had been made for official posts to cover a much larger territory – this applied to civil service jobs and the professional trades as well as to the broad masses of the urban and country poor. There were actually something approaching three million people who scarcely owned more than the shirt on their back, and who had to be content with a miserably-paid six-month job in agriculture before an important industry had taken root and grown to any size in the essentially agrarian territory which was all that remained of the former Greater Hungary.

While the farmer received preposterously low returns on his surplus corn, industrial products reaped a higher reward, as a result of the indispensable protective duties, a lack of domestic raw materials, and the loss of the only seaport the country had had: Fiume, on the Adriatic. A blatant discrepancy existed between payment for the only items which were available in abundance (wheat, wine and fruit), and the high prices that were demanded for industrial raw materials in a country which was without forests, metals, coal, hydroelectric power sources or petroleum reserves, not to mention raw materials for the textile industry. There could be only one result: unemployment, hunger and severe hardship for individual members of the community, and well-nigh insuperable difficulties for state organs to perform social tasks which were crying out for a satisfactory solution. To top it all, the global financial crisis affected every country at the beginning of the 1930s, and brought misfortune even to those whose fragile financial foundations held little hope for material progress.

The fact that Hungary nonetheless emerged from its trials and tribulations more or less unscathed was in no small way due to the far-sighted and skilful management of affairs by Count Belthen, as the head of government. He exercised a firm hand on policies, and his regime was in many people's minds

– if not formally yet in fact – little short of dictatorial. With the three hostile nations forming the so-called 'Little Entente' flanking the northern, eastern and southern borders, and on the fourth side the considerably weakened Austria, racked with internal disputes, in such a situation Bethlen's foreign policy was bound to turn elsewhere for support. Since Britain and France showed an almost criminally negligible interest, there was really only one other country possible to approach: Italy.

Mussolini had already created a regime worthy of respect before he was seized by megalomania, and on the slippery slope of his Abyssinian adventure hurled his beautiful country over the precipice into a World War. There was the prospect for Hungary of a fruitful collaboration, at least in the economic sphere, further enhanced by *Il Duce*'s manifest personal sympathy for the sorely mutilated Magyar republic. This sentiment may have been based on purely emotional considerations, but in all probability it had something to do with the notion that Italy too had been wronged when the war ended. Not through the loss of territory, as was the case with Hungary, but rather through its expectations of truly large conquests having been thwarted. Mussolini's famous words 'Treaties are not meant to last for ever!' were embossed in letters of gold on the memorial column in Liberty Square in Budapest, where the national flag fluttered at half-mast and four statues symbolised the lost territories in the north and the south, and the east and the west. They were to remind the Hungarian people, year after year, of all they had been deprived of through the machinations of foreign Powers, but which they always hoped to regain, either by Dame Fortune's happy intervention or by their own efforts.

Bethlen was too wise, however, to put his faith in Italian loyalty alone. Instead he turned in the direction where his great predecessor Count István Szechenyi, 100 years previously, had established valuable connections: Great Britain. Hungary was in the position of having a keen ally and loyal champion in the British newspaper magnate Lord Rothermere. The same year (1927) that Bethlen concluded his friendship pact with Italy,

Rothermere began an extensive press campaign demanding a revision of the Treaty of Trianon. Gradually a special cross-party group – the Friends of Hungary – was formed in the British parliament, with something like fifty members. If matters had developed, and been allowed to develop, in an undisturbed manner, it is not unlikely that Hungary would have adopted a different and far happier course than that which was the case over the decade that followed. At the very climax of his long political career, however, and still some way off his sixtieth birthday, Bethlen appears to have quite suddenly tired of steering the nation following his ten tough years as head of government. Perhaps because he had had enough of the bickering and quarrelling of the lower house of parliament, he returned to private life, leaving much unfinished work behind. It was generally believed among those in the know that, after a reasonably short period of rest, he would return to the leadership and resume the tasks he had prematurely abandoned. Fate, however, would have it otherwise.

Allow me here, dear reader, parenthetically, to mention the fact that it is just at this moment in time – 1931 – that my own small private affairs brought me into closer contact with this country, a country I have got to know exceedingly well and become extremely fond of. One chance meeting a generation earlier and now another. Travelling from the south towards Moscow, I met in Budapest a friend (who has since passed away) called Deszsö Bayer-Krucsay, the Swedish consul-general and a man with a number of influential acquaintances in leading circles. When he heard that I was contemplating the idea of publishing a book entitled *Through Yugoslavia on Horseback*, a parallel to a work on Russia from my youth, and seeing that the chances were slim of the project ever materialising, he suggested shifting the scene to his own native country, Hungary.

'Just decide the date', he said, 'and I'll have everything prepared: official approval, two military horses and a Hungarian travelling companion, necessary since you still don't have full command of our language!'

Well, why not? We agreed on two months from then – it was 19 May, a date that had had special importance in my life for the past two decades. I bade farewell and left together with my wife for Moscow, where the capricious hand of Fate, in the form of a cavalry general, by the name of Budënny and later appointed Marshal of the Soviet Union and First Deputy Commissar for Defence, was to make a similar offer: repeating the exploits of my youth, *Through Russia on Horseback*, following the same route, only a generation later. It was a tempting proposition, but perhaps a trifle adventurous for someone soon to be in his sixties.

I therefore declined his kind offer with many thanks, while precisely on 19 July I got into the saddle for a thousand-kilometre ride through Hungary. All I will say here about that ride is that it gave me a cross-sectional insight into Hungarian society, something I couldn't have achieved better in any other way within the space of a couple of months. Once back in Budapest, I remained there for a full fourteen years, and was able, in my position as university lecturer, consular assistant and eventually office employee when our embassy moved in 1938, to follow political and social developments at close hand. Thereby I was able to do my share in strengthening both the cultural and economic relations between our two countries. Plus, most recently, perform tasks of a not-insignificant nature: the Swedish Red Cross charity work in 1944 and 1945.

But let us return to the political situation in the country and its development. The Minister of Defence, Gyula Gömbös, who had played quite a prominent role in the promotion of a national consciousness after 1919, now took over governmental responsibility. It was 1932, and until he was stricken down by a fatal illness at the age of fifty, he managed over a period of four years to forge a rather shaky basis upon which Hungary could recover some of its lost territories. Sadly, however, this helped to pave the way for the country's final woeful destiny.

The starting point was the unfortunate Jewish issue. When friends back home during those years asked me about the situation, I would say ironically that in Hungary there live 6 per cent Jews, 94 per cent anti-Semites, and me, who am neither of the aforementioned. It was plainly an exaggeration of the anti-Semitic issue, but if my reply didn't exactly hit the nail on the head, it wasn't all that far off. In this context I will merely mention a single example from my own experience.

Every autumn there were anti-Semitic demonstrations among the students at the university. These took place on a regular basis in November, when student life had got going, so to speak, after the new batch of students had been registered. I was compelled personally to escort to the lecture hall one or two Jewish students to prevent them from being mobbed by their so-called Christian classmates. It all ended up by classes being suspended for a week or two and the university being closed until such time as heated emotions had subsided. The issue at stake was the fact that the maximum percentage of Jewish students admitted had been exceeded; the academic *numerus clausus* in current use stipulated that the figure should not exceed 6 per cent, equivalent to the proportion of Jews in the Hungarian population. A complaint was lodged and forwarded to the Minister of Culture, Professor Hóman. Although himself a so-called *sváb* ('*schwaber*' in German, meaning a native of Hungary of German origin), and also an unabashed anti-Semite, he was sensible enough to give the students the following proper explanation. The complaint was justified: there were actually more than 6 per cent Jews among the total number of students, but not among the Jewish students newly enrolled, where the rule had been strictly applied. What had happened was that during the second year of studies, and then in the following years too, there were always a number of students who dropped out, more often than not for lack of funds preventing them from continuing. Not among the Jews, however, the Minister pointed out; a destitute Jew could always count on assistance from his co-religionists, while it was the Christians whose numbers were falling below the 94 per cent level. 'If we Christians', he added, 'helped each other as loyally as the Jews, the Jewish percentage would never exceed the levels prescribed in the ordinance – that's the whole point!'

He was quite right. Among my own students over the years there were a couple of the brightest Christian young men I have ever taught. On several occasions they were almost forced to abandon their studies. For me it was a source of joy and a privilege to be able to assist them. All the same, I found it very odd that in the whole of Budapest there were no native Christians willing to help their impoverished but exceedingly clever compatriots and fellow-Christians to reach the end of their studies and a successful result; it was left to a foreigner, with whom they had studied more for the pleasure of it than for personal necessity . . .

Nonetheless, it must be admitted that there were real reasons for the anti-Semitic sentiments. We Swedes have never had a burning Jewish issue to contend with, and find it somewhat difficult to adjust to the mentality of a nation in which banks and commercial enterprises, newspapers and publishing houses, wholesale and retail businesses, legal practices and the medical profession – all to a certain degree, if not to the very largest degree – lay in Jewish hands. This did not only include those Jews whose families had lived in the country for many generations and for many centuries, and who after the process of emancipation of the previous century had found themselves almost on a par with other elements in the population, and had been able to marry into Christian families to the extent that it was hardly possible to determine who was Jew and who was not. It also included those who were known as Galicians and Eastern Jews of a more dubious type who had slipped in from territories to the north in Poland and Romania in the east, and who had not been able or had not had enough time to assimilate.

The compact solidarity of the Jews has of course its historical roots in their persecution and repression, which invariably served to create a reaction from a minority who protected their own interests and even at times their own lives. They put up a solid wall to confront the efforts of rival 'Aryans' and 'Turanians' to achieve some financial gain, naturally on the presumption that the Jewish element in the population had been able to acquire a number of key positions in society. This was undoubtedly the case as far as Hungary was concerned, particularly following Werkele's liberal reforms at the end of the nineteenth century. On the other hand, however, there is every reason to wonder how it was ever possible that the 94 per cent of so-called 'Aryan' citizens, who still enjoyed the prerogative of pretty well all civil service jobs and military posts, allowed themselves to be pushed into second place by a small minority belonging to another race – it wasn't so much a matter of religion, as the anti-Semitism in its purest form made no difference between what our law terms as 'members of the Mosaic creed' and loyal Christian Jews who had entirely ceased to regard themselves as Jews.

The explanation is simpler than it might at first appear. In part it lies in the fact that, as implied above, there existed a false sense of solidarity and collaboration among the Christian elements in the population, which in Hungary are split between the powerful Catholic Church and the two or three Protestant churches together with the various other denominations. The explanation may also partly be found in another situation which was roughly contemporary with Hungary's development. When the Afrikaans-speaking Boers in South Africa refused to grant the British immigrants full civil rights, plunging South Africa at the turn of the century into a wasteful and disastrous conflict, they seemed to have forgotten that if you sell your land to another, you must be prepared to accept the consequences.

I do not wish to pass too harsh a judgment, but I venture to suggest that while the Hungarian people at a similar point in time appeared to be heading for a happy and splendid future, during the following quarter of a century they largely sold their right of primogeniture. And for not much more than peanuts ... Quoting the Bible, when Esau wanted to live a life of luxury while Jacob toiled away in drudgery, he eventually lost both his position and his influence as well as his future, and Jacob still had a trump up his sleeve. Hungarian aristocrats and the country nobility (who wasn't a 'noble' in Hungary at that time, save the peasants and the Jews?) were not too fond of work but wished to live well and have a 'position' – preferably a well-paid sinecure – which by means of *Onkelwirtschafft* (my own term for pulling strings and having friends in high places) was fairly easy to obtain after three years' study for a Doctor of Law degree. Again, the Jew is not only shrewd and clever as Jacob was, or perhaps dishonest as his uncle and father-in-law Laban; he is above all industrious, thrifty and for the most part gifted – as far as integrity in general conduct and dealings is concerned, the two communities were more or less similar. The Jew 'goes about his business well', to coin a phrase. Anti-Semitic friends of mine, when asked why with their attitude they still frequently chose to make their purchases in Jewish shops, sometimes replied that 'there were no others', and sometimes quite openly – and with a little embarrassment – admitted that they were better served, more rapidly and more reliably, than in non-Jewish shops!

Furthermore, people were prepared to sell themselves for ready cash. How many estates were transferred into the hands of the clever, workmanlike Jewish bailiff because a lazy landowner with a taste for the good life found himself deeper and deeper in debt as expenses outweighed income and he was forced to abandon home and property! And how many bigwigs within the aristocracy or the world of politics and the civil service did not loan a name like 'Christenschild' to a number of Jewish businesses in exchange for a fee and a few board meetings a year! What was expected of them in return, and what they were obliged to give if they wished to continue their comfortable and leisurely living, was just the odd favourable word or two when the Jewish firm required a licence or a franchise. They had sold themselves and had to accept the consequences. If they refused, it was not merely a case of saying goodbye to the free-and-easy life and its pleasures; they would be losing influence over what they had paid for in pure gold, and they stood the risk of being boycotted in those fields of activity where Jews more often than not had most say.

This rather wordy analysis may perhaps be of some use in

assessing Hungarian politics in the 1930s. Gömbös was, as
already stated, a convinced anti-Semite, and belonged to a
category of people known in that part of the world as
Rassenschützler, that is, keen proponents of the superiority of
the Aryan race. In his foreign policy he unfortunately was not
content with following his predecessor's Italian orientation,
which through Mussolini's courtship of Britain and France in
order to protect Austria's independence might have led to the
formation of a block to hinder German aspirations in the East,
and thus be of vital importance for the future. He chose to go
in another direction. When the *Führer* found in the Jewish
issue a satisfactory platform for National-Socialist propaganda
and for consolidating his grip on the German people, Gömbös
soon got tangled in Hitler's web. Admittedly, the pact signed
in Rome in 1934 with Italy and Austria – the so-called 'Rome
Protocol' – implied a guarantee of the *status quo* in the Danube
Basin against German plans of annexation, and the friendship
with Austria got into full swing with a remarkable show of
coquetry in favour of the little anti-Nazi dictator Dollfuss, who
was given a rousing welcome on his visit to Budapest.
Developments soon took a different course, however. Dollfuss
was killed in July 1934 in one of the most macabre assassinations in world history, while for his part Mussolini fell
victim to a bout of megalomania in crushing Abyssinia in an
orgy of wasted money and spilt blood.

Instead of distancing himself from such methods, and
contributing to the League of Nations' sanctions against Italy
alongside most of the civilised world, Gömbös trod another
path which, following the forging of the German–Italian axis,
gradually led Hungary by the nose straight into their power.
Mussolini's dreams of a revival of a Roman Empire encom-
passing the Mediterranean Sea – completely counter to
Western Powers' interests – had led him into involvement in
the Spanish Civil War, and into linking the Fascist movement
with German Nazism. Thus Austria was left to its fate, and
Hungary was compelled to suffer the consequences of its
collaboration with Hitlerism, which Gömbös, now dead, had

failed to envisage, even more so than Bethlen. The country's politics was now for an unpredictable time to come tied to that of the two big authoritarian Axis Powers; Hungary could expect little sympathy to be shown by the Western democracies for its pathetic demands for a revision of the Treaty of Trianon.

For a while it seemed as though the Hungarians had backed the right horse. As a by-product of Hitler's violent annexation of Austria and Czechoslovakia as part of Greater Germany, Hungary obtained a gift in the form of a slice of Slovakian territory lost in the 1920 peace process, and the following winter marched into what was known as the Carpathian-Russian province in the north-east and took possession of it. In exchange, 'all' that was required of Hungary was an alliance with the German–Japanese–Italian anti-Comintern Pact and withdrawal from the League of Nations, as well as, last but not least, turning a blind eye when Germany began its infamous invasion of Poland in the autumn of 1939. It was not so easy to keep a straight face then after all the enthusiastic assurances of eternal friendship that were showered over this country when the recovery of these Carpathian-Russian territories gave Hungary a common border with Poland, always a popular neighbour since ancient times. The only thing one could be happy about was the fact that the Hungarians did not actually have to take part in the butchery.

Give a dictator an inch and he'll take a mile. When Italy, plainly willing to wait a while and see which way the wind was blowing, abandoned its 'non-belligerent' status the following summer and for its own specific purposes took advantage of the situation that had arisen with Germany's violation of five independent countries' sovereignty in Western Europe and its plot together with the Soviet Union to carve up Poland, a fresh chance appeared for Hungary to recover further territory. The so-called Viennese Arbitration process in the autumn of 1940 allowed Hungary to reclaim the north-eastern corner of Siebenbrüggen with its mixed Hungarian–Romanian population. Nothing is obtained free of charge in this sordid world of ours. The cost, paid in November, was Hungary's forced alliance with the 'Pact of Steel' involving Germany, Italy and Japan, of fatal significance for the future.

I can personally vouch for the fact that it was not a voluntary step, at least as far as the Hungarian head of state was concerned. On the occasion of an audience I had had with the Regent in a completely different context, he had in full confidence and unreservedly expressed his sincere desire to mediate a peace between the warring parties. Such a mediation might then just have been possible, particularly if efforts had been channelled through our King and the Holy See – King Gustav and the Pope exerted an authority which was not to be dismissed. I dared pray, sincerely and respectfully, that for the sake of God and the people and the history of the world this opportunity should not be missed. It is not difficult to imagine with what pangs of conscience he was later compelled to quash these hopes, hopes which, had they been fulfilled, would have seen his name inscribed in letters of gold in the annals of history.

The then Prime Minister, Count Teleki, a scientist and man of honour of impeccable conduct, who for local patriotic reasons (he also hailed from Siebenbrüggen) had actively worked towards the reinstatement of that region in the national territory, had also with a heavy heart seen how his country more and more became chained to the Hitlerite triumphal chariot of fire. A few months later he was to give substantial proof of this. Towards the end of March 1941 his decision *not* to go along with the joint German–Italian destruction of the Yugoslav state, which had only recently entered into a treaty of friendship with Hungary, cost him his life. His successor, Foreign Minister Bárdossy, felt no qualms over such scruples, and even cashed in on the situation: after barely two weeks Hungarian troops were able to march in and take possession of the northernmost parts of their southern neighbour. This was the fourth, and last, strip of land regained by Hungary, bringing the territory recovered since the disastrous peace treaty of 1919 up to almost half the original land lost. Nobody knew then that this was one of the last nails in the thousand-year-old Hungarian kingdom's coffin, although its fate was not finally sealed until the German declaration of war on the Soviet Union on 22 June 1941.

A Hungarian declaration of war followed almost immediately afterwards, but was preceded by a small incident of considerable interest. From a reliable source I have heard that when the diplomat instructed to deliver the declaration of war to People's Commissar Molotov in Moscow arrived, the latter advised him in a friendly manner to withdraw the declaration: 'We have no quarrel with your country . . .' Not until after a hasty exchange of telegrams with Bárdossy was the Hungarian diplomat obliged to obey orders and formally compel the Russian to accept the fateful document.

Relations were broken off, and by chance it fell to me as a Russian speaker to escort the Russian embassy staff out of Budapest towards Istanbul – Sweden had been selected as the protective power for Soviet interests in Hungary. To the Hungarians' credit it must be said that in all probability never have the representatives of a hostile foreign power been interned and treated in such a chivalrous and pleasant manner as the Russians were on this occasion in Budapest and on their way to their chosen destination. Our splendid young *chargé d'affaires*, Nils Montan, decided to request a certificate to this effect from the head of the Russian embassy, Charonov, and a very appreciative acknowledgement of Hungarian behaviour was given. When the Russians finally departed from the Haidarpascha railway station outside Istanbul, that acknowledgement was again given to me, this time verbally in the most flattering terms.

So now in 1941 – as in 1914 – the Hungarian people were at war, without having been consulted in the matter, and most certainly contrary to their innermost desires, driven there by the mighty tide of events. There followed what must clearly be seen as a ridiculous declaration of war on Great Britain and the United States of America. Was this inspired by feelings of hatred towards the Russian and British people? Surely not. Did the Hungarians have a bone to pick with the

Americans? Even less justified: about one-tenth of all Hungarians was an immigrant, or a child of one, in the USA. Yet a meaningless declaration of war on the Big Country the other side of the Atlantic had to be made, because that was the desire of Herr Hitler.

The Hungarian army was of little significance, and poorly equipped, and had an inexperienced leadership – scarcely three years had passed since it had officially been established. A few divisions were launched against Russia and performed their tasks dutifully. Young officers returning on leave, however, told me of the embarrassment they felt when soldiers up at the River Don front would ask them in idle moments: 'Please, lieutenant, tell me, what are we doing here really, 2,000km from our village where everything's in a mess with us men away from home? Are *we* meant to conquer Russia? We neither can nor want to . . . ' Nor did the Russians wish *them* any harm at that point in time. A young lieutenant on the reserve list, who had been one of my students learning Swedish, and who up at the front learnt passable Russian, later shared his experiences with me. A small unit was busy repairing a road together with a large detachment of German soldiers when one night they were surrounded by Russians and taken prisoner. They were lined up and all the Germans pulled out and immediately shot. The Hungarians were to learn their fate the following morning at 8.00am 'What a frightful night that must have been for you!' I muttered. 'Oh no, not all that bad', my student replied. 'Since we had been spared, there had to be some meaning behind it . . . ' And so it was. After they had been lined up afresh in the morning, the Soviet officer explained that they were being released and could now make their way home westwards, towards Budapest. 'You know where it is and you know the way there, since you got here in the first place!' came the wryly humorous comment.

It was mid-winter and 1,500km to the Hungarian border. The lieutenant was impudent enough to blurt out: 'We had three sleighs with us when we came and plenty of food, which you've taken from us. How shall we ever get home?' He got a sleigh back and sufficient bread and meat for his men to last a few days.

The main body of the Hungarian army, however, came to grief, when 80,000 men were trapped in a narrow pocket of land at Voronjesj: a quarter of them died on the battlefield, and the remainder were listed as missing or captured. In their attempt to retreat from the pincer movement the supply forces' vehicles were destroyed and their fuel went up in smoke – the rearguard had panicked and, oblivious to the fate of their fellow troops, had tried to hinder the pursuing enemy as much as possible.

This, then, was the state of the war for Hungary in January 1942. Later in the year there were German successes in south-east Russia and in North Africa, although a stop was put to them at Stalingrad and El Alamein. In the early autumn, however, it was fairly clear that the main objectives – the Suez Canal and the oilfields at Baku – would never be attained. I myself made my own little forecast that the war would be over within a couple of years – I couldn't see us having to put up with a sixth winter of warfare. There I was wrong – it turned out to be the most dreadful of them all, but it was also the last. Victory had actually already begun to slip through the fingers of the European powers of the Pact of Steel. Their chances of success now lay only in the Far East, and in the Pacific. When and how nobody could tell.

The role played by the Hungarian army from now on was very much a secondary one. A few divisions were allotted here and there to various German army groups while others were dispatched as garrisons to the Ukraine, where in general they incurred the hatred of the local population, being guilty of a series of abuses. Considerable forces were also sent to the border with Romania. Both countries had joined the Axis almost simultaneously, but mutually harboured the fiercest suspicions towards each other over disputed border areas. They both hoped that in the final outcome they would be able to seize this entire territory for themselves. This endeavour to regain lost territory became one more of the fetters chaining

Hungary to Hitler's Germany in the unrelenting march towards ultimate destruction.

In the meantime the domestic political scene was marked by the situation prevailing in the mighty neighbouring country to the west. The Jewish question – in other words – was pushed more and more to the fore. An indirect consequence of the German assault on Poland was the strengthening of anti-Semitic currents. Huge numbers of Orthodox Jews streamed over the border in their flight from the Nazis; impoverished, unkempt, scheming and miserly (in the popular perception at that time), they formed an unwelcome feature even for their kindred spirits among the resident Jewish community. The call for stricter laws against them grew louder. The Hungarian Nazi movement, which under the sign of the Arrow Cross wanted to keep abreast of the German movement and its swastika, began to secretly recruit supporters – within the army, among other institutions – in addition to those who had joined one of the previously very divided factions quite openly. In more sensible and intelligent circles it was thought that one could afford to treat these people as a bit of a joke so long as their few representatives in parliament were split into various 'parties' under different names. Gradually, however, it became evident that they had to be taken seriously. In the autumn of 1940 their most prominent leader, the ex-Major Ferenc Szálasi, who had served a prison sentence for subversive activities and been released under an amnesty, had succeeded in uniting the various groups, racked with mutual suspicion and envy, into a single organisation committed to the cause of German Nazism.

This now quite naturally became the stronghold of national anti-Semitism, and cashed in on the mounting hostility towards the Jews. Count Teleki had previously been called upon to steer the first of the anti-Jewish laws through parliament, a law based on religious issues rather than racial discrimination. A couple of years later came the second law, considerably sharper in tone and content, and following heated parliamentary debates a third was pushed through in which the racial issue formed the basis of the new regulations. With this law practically every person defined as a Jew became a second-class citizen, deprived of some of the most basic civil rights. The Arrow Cross had already by then scored their first big political success. A parliamentary group with a con-stitutional, non-revolutionary basis but extreme right-wing tendencies was formed under the leadership of the former Prime Minister Béla Imrédy. A highly competent economist, but politically short-sighted and inexperienced as well as being an unrestrained religious fanatic, Imrédy was in point of fact the instigator of Jewish persecution as head of government in 1938–9. Ironically enough, fate would have it that while it was he who had had the first anti-Jewish law woven together, it was also he who became its most notable victim. Before the law had been passed and had time enough to be applied, he tripped over a particularly irritating stumbling-block: his opponents were able to demonstrate that he himself had Jewish blood in his veins, and to avoid the ridicule of the general public he was forced to step down.

All the more bitter, then, was his struggle as leader of the opposition. After he had combined the forces of his own personal and quite numerous group of anti-Semitic supporters with those of Szálasi's Arrow Cross, this united front of what in Hungary came to be known as right-wing radicals became a rather embarrassing thorn in the side of the Centre Party, which was in power at that time. Even if it never became strong enough to take the reins of government by legal means, this united front still gained a large measure of popularity, especially within the military and the student movement.

When Count Teleki's successor as head of government, Bárdossy, after barely a year in office and not a very happy year at that, was induced to leave the government 'for reasons of health', a skilful opportunist of unimpeachable repute, Miklós Kállay, took his place. His none too easy job was to pilot the ship of state through the troubled German waters and in consideration of the understandable demands of national interests, which he achieved with a remarkable flexibility. His methods involved siding with the left and siding with the right, by turns, and in initiated circles they earned him the political nomenclature of *'Kállay kettös'* – the Kállay two-step! By the use of delaying tactics and emergency measures he was able to soften the impact of the anti-Jewish laws and still avoid annoying the Germans unduly, while undoubtedly reaching out to Britain and the US, and perhaps the Russians too. Had he been able to remain at the helm, he might have managed to steer to smoother waters where Hungary's small craft need not have suffered the horrendous shipwrecks which finally sank the German and Italian colossi, and ultimately the Japanese too.

On Sunday 19 March 1944 (why do almost all revolutions, regicides and imperial assassinations occur in the month of March?) proof was given that the Germans knew perfectly well just where they had Hungary's head of state as well as the best part of his government. They took the matter resolutely into their own hands, while continuing to play the game with Hungarian marionettes. With incredible speed and precision, and after meticulous preparation, they carried out their coup, and the curtain went up on the tragedy which would be played out in the course of the year, and reach its climax at the New Year 1945 with the final hours of a 1,000-year-old kingdom.

THE FIRST ACT:

The Deportation of the Jews

A ROUND six o'clock on a Sunday morning in the early spring of 1944 a vast number of aircraft could be seen swarming over the city of Budapest. No alarm was heard, no bombs were dropped.

Practice flights performed by Hungarian squadrons?

No, the planes were German – with swastikas. What were they doing here, with no visible enemy around, and why were they circling round and round and round, and not returning to where they had come from? Nobody could say, but evidently something was brewing.

My telephone rang at eight o'clock – did I know what was going on? Not the slightest idea, but it certainly looked damned strange . . .

Half an hour later the explanation arrived. A Hungarian newspaperman had the information – 'The entire city is overrun by Germans. They've taken command of police headquarters, the General Post Office, telegraph and radio stations. Long columns of German military vehicles are scouring the streets. The Palace and the Ministry buildings up on the hill are under German guard, patrols are out arresting all the political leaders who have shown little or no sympathy for the Germans. Mainly they're after people of Jewish descent and liberal attitudes.'

And the Regent?

He had been invited to visit Hitler, who wished to persuade him to promise to make available a large Hungarian army contingent, and he should have been back on the Saturday. On the way home, however, some hindrance had 'regrettably' prevented His Excellency from continuing his journey until the following day.

During this time German tanks and lorries had sped over the border straight for Budapest, a distance they covered in a couple of hours. When Horthy was finally released and reached the capital, he found it already 'kidnapped' as Copenhagen had been in April 1940. Our mighty 'ally's' tactics had been well rehearsed in the assaults on Denmark and Norway, and the Germans' widely celebrated striking power and organisational capacity did not fail to meet expectations this time either. The choice of day could not have been better, either: Sunday, the day of rest in government offices and ministries, at least for those whose boss was not tipped off in advance of the plot; out of a dozen or so ministers there were at least four or five reliably sympathetic to the German cause, whom it was not necessary to render harmless. The remainder were pulled in with unerring precision by the Gestapo, which had taken immediate possession of police headquarters and other essential detention centres, and had set up its own centre of operations in a couple of well-appointed hotels up at Schwabenberg on the Buda side. Prime Minister Kállay was able to reach safety at the very last minute in the Turkish embassy, where he was protected by extraterritorial immunity but was unable to confer with the Head of State as the telephone had naturally been cut off.

Within a few hours the Germans were certain that no highly-placed official remained in the civil and military administrations capable of joining a popular revolt against the occupying power, or who had not immediately gained a secure hiding place. At the Palace, surrounded by German troops, the Regent's hands were firmly tied by threats of bombardment and destruction of the capital unless he agreed to appoint a new government, clearly in line with German wishes. In order to avoid bloodshed and the risk of a civil war, he found himself forced to yield to these demands, most probably in the hope that, remaining at his post, he could better serve the country rather than by burning his boats and allowing himself to be carted off to Germany as a prisoner.

A few days later the composition of the new government – thus arrived at in 'legal' form – was made known. General Sztólay, the Hungarian envoy in Berlin, was appointed both head of government and the now largely unimportant Foreign Minister: his collaboration in the coup had probably been assured of beforehand. In order to put a suitable complexion on the whole matter – at least outwardly to satisfy Hungarian national feeling – it was decided to retain in their posts those ministers whose loyalty to the German regime could not be called into question. It was openly reported that Imrédy was urged to join the government, but that he had made conditions that were unacceptable to the Germans.

The Ministry of the Interior, of prime importance at this juncture, was handed to the former leader of the Hungarian minority in Czechoslovakia, Jaross, a marked nationalist. He had no hesitation in appointing as his Permanent Secretaries two of Hungary's wildest anti-Semites, the former gendarme Major Baky and the civil governor in Pest, Endre. Knowing something of the previous careers of these gentlemen – Endre wanted everybody who was not of pure Hungarian blood chased out of the regained territories, and Baky was considered to be even worse – it was not difficult to work out that what was under way was the extermination of the Jewish population, following the German pattern.

During the very first week following the coup, not only all prominent Jewish businessmen but also Jews who occupied important positions in the cultural life of the city were either arrested or deported to Germany. Similar measures were taken with the leaders of the political left, in the event they had not found a safe place abroad, as was the case with the Liberal Party boss Eckhardt and a few leading Social Democrats.

The observation was later made in some quarters that a few Hungarian regiments loyal to the government could well have outflanked the Germans and nipped the coup in the bud. But were there such regiments at hand? And even if there had been, it is difficult to see what could have been gained by such a move. The Germans had air supremacy and the element of surprise, while the Russian steamroller in the east was still an immense distance away, and what there was of a Hungarian army lay mostly at different points along the German frontline; the border guard would hardly risk leaving its positions at Siebenbürgen for fear that the Romanians would seize the opportunity to immediately occupy the territory, which could then never be recovered. In addition to which corps commanders and officers in general were invariably either pro-German and secret members of the Arrow Cross, or they were indecisive. The army lacked leaders capable of inspiring others to join a resistance movement of any size. The cunning calculation which had provided the country with what was formally a fully legal government would have meant that any armed revolt was interpreted as just that – open revolt – and would have led to the risk of those involved being tried for treason should it fail. No such bold venture was on the cards.

The government had the support of the enormous war machine provided by the Germans. Knowledge of what had happened to the Poles and the Yugoslavs, the Belgians and the Dutch, the Danes and the Norwegians, was depressing enough for a small, under-equipped nation, which was also split and disunited. No aid was to be expected from the West, and Russian help at that point in time was not to be thought of. Matters would have to take their course, and it turned out to be anything but pleasant.

Endre and Baky were not slow to move. The systematic persecution and total annihilation of the entire Jewish population – only the capital's broad masses were spared for the moment – started as early as April, and proceeded along two routes. One of them, for which Endre was responsible, was the setting-up of fenced-in Jewish ghettoes in the larger provincial cities, with the aim of concentrating all Jews in one place where they could be dealt with in an entirely arbitrary fashion. The other, led by Baky and employing his newly-hired gendarmes as executioners, was the deportation to Germany of hundreds of thousands of Jews.

For the moment, however, this latter procedure – which also included the confiscation of all real and personal property as well as clothing and food – was restricted to the countryside, where it was far easier to deport people than in the capital, the Jewish population of which numbered a quarter of a million. These were left in peace for the time being, probably because immediate removal would have met with insuperable practical difficulties. Besides, it was obviously feared that too much attention abroad coupled with possible riots in Budapest itself might be the result if this huge mass of people (approximately one-fifth of the city's population) were to be transported out of the country in hundreds of overcrowded railway trains.

Instead, another – let us call it – 'preparatory' expedient was found. The order was issued for every Jew who had reached six years of age to wear a fully visible 'Star of David' – a large, six-pointed yellow star, made according to a set size, sewn on the left side of the chest. The first failure to comply with the order brought a heavy fine; a repetition generally led to deportation. The wretched system of informers which immediately began to flourish – in a way which even took the Germans by surprise – meant that it was a dangerous thing even to poke your nose outside your house without wearing the star. A close friend of ours, a well-known Christian literary man, who committed this terrible crime, was at once reported and convicted. After being notified he duly made for the police station to pay off the fine personally. He has never been seen since; in a roundabout way we managed to find out that he had been taken to an internment camp on the German border, but every attempt to get him freed was frustrated. There were other instances in which little children in a family would observe the 'decorative' star on the adults' clothing and burst out: 'Mummy, when can we get a pretty little star on our clothes like the one you've got?'

In point of fact, of course, the star amounted to a sign showing that the person in question belonged to a despised class of people, persecuted as an outcast. This was naturally wholly detestable to everyone who had to put up with it, but most of all perhaps for the vast number of people with Jewish blood who fell under the category defined by the law as 'considered to be Jews', but who right from early infancy had been baptised and admitted to the Christian faith. These people, who would never have thought of themselves as Jewish and who had never had anything to do with the Jewish religious community, felt deeply offended at having to give the outward appearance of being Jewish, and were often prepared to receive punishment rather than bear a mark which distinguished them as belonging to a race of pariahs. They frequently managed to avoid identification, however, particularly if their physical appearance did not resemble that of the classic image of a Jew, even though we are talking here of a society where dark-complexioned people with dark hair and eyes were the norm. They could be fortunate enough to move around for weeks at a time without being accosted, unless an informer had been busy and had alerted the authorities.

The extent to which this informer activity had spread across the country can be shown by the following example. A domestic servant of Polish origin, who was in my employ as well as in that of several other homes in the inner city, but who lived far out in the suburbs, told me that she was repeatedly approached by neighbouring housewives wondering whether, knowing as she did so many of the 'better families', she couldn't supply them with names and addresses of any of the Jews so they could report them to the proper authorities. Either these hyenas were hoping for some economic recompense, a prize per head, or that their intervention would bring them prestige and render them unimpeachable. We found this standard of behaviour more nefarious even than the persecution itself of entirely innocent people, whose only offence was to allow themselves to be born of wholly or half-Jewish parents.

My own excellent chauffeur, a particularly skilful mechanic, who had previously served as chauffeur at the embassy but who had been called up for national service two years back, was a case in point. Under no circumstances did he wish to travel around in my car with a yellow star pinned to his chest, and through the assistance of several generals of my acquaintance I was able to exclude him from further service of this nature. On the other hand he was threatened now with punishment and deportation if he were reported and denounced by a colleague whose malevolent nature we were only too aware of. Some means of saving his skin and that of his family and getting him out of the country was now urgently needed. Remarkable to say, the plan we formulated was successful. He had a sister, a young widow with two small children, who lived far out in the country. In the utmost secrecy my wife drove her into town via a series of adventure-packed routes, and we managed to get the whole family – the chauffeur was married and his wife was expecting – together with other *protégés* into a transport column which finally made it across into Switzerland, where the new 'world citizen' later saw the light of day. A particularly crafty and skilful Zionist had bribed his German connections to permit safe passage to Palestine for no fewer than 1,700 Jews who, according to the agreement, were to be shipped along the Danube to the estuary and by sea to their destination. Negotiations went on for weeks, and in the end the would-be refugees were dumped on a train and landed up in . . . Hanover! They were held there in an internment camp – the now-infamous Belsen – for several months, until the bribed Germans, to their credit, kept their word and had the entire transport ferried group by group over the border to Switzerland. They were given a friendly welcome there, and could thank their lucky stars they had escaped the most dreadful place of all: the extermination camps in the Polish General Government.

After the regime change described later in this book in the 'Intermezzo' chapter, the order to wear the yellow star was somewhat relaxed and many Jews stopped wearing it. Following the Arrow Cross coup on 15 October, however, they paid bitterly for this neglect when entire buildings where Jews lived had to be equipped with a large yellow star placed above the doorway. If they ventured out of doors, or had been brazen enough to dispose of their racial symbol and were identified as Jews, they were immediately in mortal danger.

For deportation purposes huge concentration camps were put into operation, often in open brick-walled barns or under the open sky exposed to wind, rain and cold. The wretched people were shoved into sealed cattle trucks in long goods trains under a rain of kicks and blows, treatment not even reserved for cattle, pigs and sheep. Men and women, the elderly, and small and older children, were squeezed in – sixty, seventy or eighty to a wagon – as long as there was an inch of room to spare, whereupon the sliding doors were fastened and locked. No allowance was made for food and water, let alone for relieving themselves during the long days and nights the hellish trip took *en route* to the 'Ostmark' or the Polish General Government. I fortunately was spared the sight of such a train, but unbiased witnesses abound and are so many in number that further confirmation is superfluous.

The following observation may be of some interest, however. Reliable sources claim that amazement was expressed in German quarters over the state in which the deportees were found when they were unloaded in Vienna for further transport to their respective work locations. Some had to be dragged out dead, others' hair had turned white and they had lost their reason owing to the horrors of their journey – the entire picture offered a scene of human misery exceeding anything the wildest fantasy could conjure up. Food and drink were now available, since it was a matter of having slaves fit for work in the production of essential items for the war industry – but what sort of use were these human rags!

This was in Vienna. In the Polish General Government matters were somewhat simpler. There the cargo, dead or alive, was carted off to the extermination camps of Auschwitz and Birkenau. The ingenious construction of these camps permitted the instantaneous putting to death of the victims by gas emitted from the showers, and further transport of the naked corpses by rail to the cremation ovens. The daily killing capacity at just one of these institutions was reported as 6,000. . .

In my capacity as the Swedish embassy's consultant on Jewish affairs, I was provided with a complete layout of the installations and accurate figures concerning transportation of people. When at the beginning of May the figure had reached 60,000 and in a report home to the Swedish foreign office I wanted to quote this figure, the head of the department reacted by claiming that this figure was undoubtedly far in excess of reality, and it was reduced by two-thirds. To check, I sought out an officer attached to the Hungarian general staff whose job was to distribute the 300,000-strong male Jewish workforce which the Hungarian government had reserved the right to dispose of for its own needs in road repairs and construction. He was an amiable man, who did his best to save the situation, and who was extraordinarily well informed about the entire nasty business.

'Is my figure mistaken?' I asked quite simply.

'Yes, it is,' was the reply, 'although don't subtract but instead add on another 20,000 so it'll be right up to date. And then you can go on adding 24,000 for each week . . . '

Towards the middle of May a report did the rounds to the effect that the British had requested the Hungarian government via the Swiss embassy to put an end to these atrocities; otherwise reprisals were threatened. When asked, Jaeger, the ambassador – generally regarded as Hitler-friendly – stated that 'this was something he hadn't heard about until now'; an exceedingly diplomatic reply, which was interpreted as a denial but in reality said nothing about the point at issue. Three days later the British intervention was known at international level, although not a word was said about it in the state-controlled Hungarian press. The reprisals took the shape of intensive air-raids for a time, even if it was to be even heavier later on – Sztójay, if he is still alive, will doubtless be paying atonement. As far as we were concerned, the incident made it clear to us what sort of individual this Jaeger was.

By 19 May, two months to the day since the coup began in

March, the world situation was such that the people governing Hungary believed themselves to be on the winning side in backing the Axis powers – the threat of reprisals did not mean any special measures need be taken . . .

For purely personal reasons which do not need to be related here, my wife and I came around to thinking that the Swedish Red Cross, with its universally high reputation, might have the advantage of being able to intervene in some way or other. It was at this point in time that Count Folke Bernadotte was appointed vice-chairman of the organisation, and it was supposed that he would take over the post as head since the highly-respected chairman, advanced in years and replete with honours and achievements, gave it to be understood that he would soon be happy to hand over the reins to younger hands.

From statements he had made in the past it was evident that Count Bernadotte was not a man to put off till tomorrow what he could do today, or at least did not delay taking action until events made it unavoidable. It did not seem to us inconceivable that he could be persuaded to accept an invitation to Hungary to look into the possibility of initiating a neutral aid pro-gramme, before the exchange of victims and related assistance became the first priority. Why wait until an intervention, in all good conscience, could no longer be delayed?

My previous dealings with the Hungarian Red Cross had provided me with an insight into the difficulties now being encountered by its social section led by an old friend of mine, Charlotte Lukács, who was also vice-president of the Board. There was any amount of work to be done, but also a serious lack of funds, and to a certain extent a lack of manpower since all those with Jewish blood had had to be dismissed. My plan – to interest Count Bernadotte in our project, and also our Swedish Red Cross, about whose work I had once given a talk for the Hungarian Red Cross organisation – was received enthusiastically. Together with '*Sarolta néni*' ('Aunt Lotte' as she was affectionately referred to by her female colleagues), I made out a rough draft of the letter of invitation.

Through my personal connections a very considerable

amount of money was placed at my disposal, and now the tricky question was how to get the Hungarian government to fall in with the idea. A possible solution – I hardly knew any of the new members of government – was provided by pure chance. A prominent lawyer, a friend of mine and former student of the Swedish language, as well as a gifted linguist and legal historian, happened to be the right-hand man of one of the ministers who had been persuaded to retain his post. He gladly took charge of preparations for me to present the plan to the general secretary of the foreign ministry, the former ambassador in Moscow and Sofia, Arnóthy-Jungert.

The idea was that at the same time the Foreign Minister would be called upon by the President of the Hungarian Red Cross, an elderly and endearing gentleman of the bureaucratic type, whose abiding characteristic was his capacity to spout his opinions rather than leap into action. He wanted to telephone the honourable member of government, something I vigorously warned against! He appeared to have no time to spare to pay a personal visit . . . On the other hand he eagerly discussed the possibility of placing the entire social section under the control of the Swedish Red Cross so that, should the war end unhappily for Hungary (God forbid!), at least the section and its property could be rescued when the army collapsed. The Red Cross in Hungary came under the supervision of the Ministry of War and was to a certain degree a state institution, which was not of course the case with our own.

On the other hand he was the kind of individual who prefers to do tomorrow what he could have done today, as well as being one of those people, difficult to handle, who cannot stick to the issue under discussion without drifting off on to immaterial and irrelevant side-issues, and then having gently to be brought back to the matter in hand. Put briefly, for all practical purposes he was fairly useless, while he had half his mind on his pretty country cottage, and in the end he had to be ruled out after a couple of costly weeks had been wasted.

The man at the foreign ministry was of another disposition. We came up against diplomatic difficulties yet again, however.

The Swedish government had not yet seen fit to give its approval to the appointment of a new Hungarian ambassador in Stockholm. Practically all of the members of the embassy had disassociated themselves from the new Hungarian regime, which was merely running the Germans' errands and which had come to power by means of a revolutionary coup.

'Let us bide our time in proceeding with your very praiseworthy plan for Swedish assistance to us until the political question has been settled,' said Jungert. 'Not until then can we begin a fruitful collaboration in the social field. And – incidentally – your country has not been particularly friendly in refusing to extend the trade agreement!'

I objected by pointing out that a courteous and pleasant gesture on the part of the Hungarians might help to smooth over relations between the two countries, and with a bit of patience we might still be able to reach a *modus vivendi* in diplomatic relations – which was in fact what happened the following month. His reply was a somewhat impatient appeal not to mix politics with social affairs.

'And how many innocent people will be led to the slaughter while we wait?' I wondered, and I implied – riskily in the circumstances but nonetheless deliberately – that for us the prime concern was the Jewish issue, even though we did of course have a broader programme for the project as a whole.

'You're mistaken,' was the answer, 'it's not as bad as it looks, and all these reports going around are very much exaggerated . . .'

And there we were again: the same denial of information which had been proved to be entirely correct.

The ground rocked beneath my feet. If I had been able to present the matter in such a way that the Jewish question was a side-issue alongside many other tasks waiting to be dealt with within the framework of Red Cross activities, the game would have been won applying the necessary diplomatic muscle. Life-long experience had taught me, however, that you often cut a poor figure if you don't lay your cards on the table at the start. In the long run it's better to go straight to the truth rather than

34

beat about the bush. Whatever the case, the conversation finished with a friendly invitation to set out my programme in writing and – surprisingly enough – to supply more details on the Jewish problem, of which it appeared neither the general secretary nor the *ministre-adjoint* knew that much about.

A couple of days later, then, I was able to produce a detailed report of the German camps where atrocities were being carried out together with a ground-plan, all of which had been obtained from a person who – by force of destiny or by God's will, whichever way you like to put it – had escaped from there. He had been given an office job by the management, and had secretly set down a number of facts and figures. A copy of the same document was also sent to our own Foreign Ministry, but whether it arrived and what sort of effect it had I do not know. In any case it appeared to leave a strong impression.

'I'll bring the matter up as soon as I can at the cabinet meeting,' said Jungert, 'but I must warn you that a transit visa for Count Bernadotte or even for his deputy through Germany will not be granted. Can't you, who have lived in this country for years and are so well acquainted with circumstances here, get yourself appointed as Swedish Red Cross delegate in Hungary, and take over leadership of the relief programme in co-operation with our own organisation?'

This was a brand-new idea, which implied a sense of responsibility and a burden possibly too heavy for a pair of shoulders already weighed down with the years and getting tired in the process. I had of course imagined being able to obtain through the proper channels a transit permit through Germany for Count Bernadotte – who after all was the nephew of King Gustav Adolf of Sweden – and prevail upon him to pay us a short visit in order to plan our activities. He would have been of invaluable help in conferring a quite different weight and authority to the start of things than would otherwise have been the case with an insignificant private person as initiator. That plan was frustrated, however, by the pitfalls of Hungarian as well as Swedish pessimism, and left me to take the matter into my own hands in order to get the operation off the ground.

Serious, unexpected obstacles reared their ugly heads right from the start. One concerned the economic aspect. Without the vice-chairman's firm support we could hardly reckon on any significant financial help from the Swedish Red Cross. We should have to look elsewhere. I did admittedly have an almost limitless source of funds at my disposal – one or two million Swiss francs, an amount ten times their worth in Hungarian *pengö*. To obtain it, however, required an extensive and time-consuming telegraph operation in code, for which our embassy considered it had no time to offer unless absolute certainty of a successful outcome could be guaranteed. Even though I was assured of receiving the money by the end of June, nothing came of my appeals. I could have cried my eyes out over the stubborn refusal.

What is more, I appeared to have suffered a crushing defeat at the hands of the Hungarian authorities. Once I had been appointed Swedish Red Cross delegate in Hungary I was granted a permit to perform humanitarian relief work – but . . . only 'within the framework of the Hungarian Red Cross's field of activity!' In the light of this organisation's official standing, in the present state of affairs any chance of coming to the help of any Jew was out of the question. It was therefore impossible to get to work on this issue – an issue which the prevailing circumstances had turned into the most urgent of tasks: namely, to save as many as possible from the horrors of deportation. The number of unfortunate people affected had risen to several hundreds of thousands during the weeks wasted in fruitless negotiations, and as the number of atrocities increased, so too did the cruelty of the methods employed.

It was essential not to lose heart. Faith moves mountains, it is said. It does provide the energy, anyway, to overcome seemingly insurmountable difficulties. There was one man in the whole of Hungary, just one, who could help me in my way forward, if he wanted to. I went straight to the office of the Regent. His aide was, I knew, an honest and kindly man; the year before he had been extremely accommodating in a matter concerning the financial interests of a Swedish woman in

Hungary and secured the consent of the Head of State in our favour – I was therefore confident that this time too he would make himself available for reasoning and argument.

My supposition proved correct. 'I will do my best by all means,' he said, ' but you are not unaware, I am sure, that His Excellency's authority is severely limited nowadays.' 'Yes, I am fully aware of this, but I wonder whether something might happen this week, if not today, in fact, which could increase his authority in some degree.' What I was referring to was the now celebrated telegram sent by King Gustav V, which was partly the result of direct appeals from a number of Jewish quarters, and partly derived from reports arriving at the Swedish foreign office. The aide smiled, gave me a knowing look, and said: *'Perhaps* you're right . . . give me a memo and I'll have it delivered on Tuesday. Call on me here on Wednesday, and we'll see!'

While the document was being handed over I risked a query: 'Didn't something happen last Saturday around 6.15pm?' 'Indeed, you are right, and have full confidence in us . . . '

A few days later a letter arrived confirming the personal intervention of the Head of State in aid of our activity irrespective of the race, religion or nationality of those it concerned. A similar letter came a further couple of days later from the Hungarian foreign office. Arnóthy-Jungert expressed a heartfelt wish that our activity would enjoy every success and 'thus contribute to the consolidation of the traditionally friendly relations between Sweden and Hungary!'

On my courtesy visit to see him I took the liberty of expressing my particular gratitude for these final words of flattery. The minister at once understood my allusion to the time he had urged me not to bring politics into the subject. With a pleasant smile he took my hand and said: 'Let's be really good friends now.' And so we became, when he himself, his wife and his son found themselves and their property in mortal danger during the Arrow Cross rampage in the late autumn. He was arrested twice, and was finally taken away as a prisoner to Germany. Before that he had had time enough to ask me to take charge of his house and seek protection for his family, which we were able to do as far as possible. It was with enormous relief that we learnt much later that he was fortunate enough to be rescued by the Allies. His delightful wife survived the partial destruction of their home and struck up a lasting friendship with us, maintaining our mutual collaboration. This is one of the many beautiful memories – among so many other dreadful ones – I have retained from those 'works and days' in Budapest.

THE SECOND ACT:

The Swedish Red Cross

AFTER six or seven weeks constantly negotiating and making use of established as well as new contacts, and exploiting the goodwill we had won all year round following the so-called 'Swedish Days' in April 1943, we finally arrived at the stage we could call 'the start'. We couldn't make up for the time that had been wasted, but it was a matter of salvaging what we could salvage. We had not, of course, sat idle but made good use of these weeks organising our activities in anticipation, always confident of ultimate success. Above all there was the need of office space, a team of colleagues and – money.

This latter preoccupation was naturally the greatest of all, after the huge amount of money I had mentioned earlier had passed me by. It derived from Jewish sources, although there was an agreement that one-tenth (in round figures some two million Hungarian *pengö*) would be used to assist non-Jews. Thus so much could have been achieved in order to come to the aid of the hundreds of thousands still left out of the almost million people belonging to the Jewish population in the country who were threatened with all kinds of danger, with hunger and with hardship.

This constant worry was alleviated in a rather unexpected way when a telegram was received announcing the imminent arrival of Raoul Wallenberg to take over as legation secretary at the Swedish embassy in charge of Jewish affairs. I immediately introduced him to our Jewish contact – attached to the Swiss embassy – who had wanted to prepare a basis for our work together broad enough that I would not have to be dependent on financial support from home. Whether Wallenberg in time came to build his exceptionally wide-ranging and beneficial activities on financial support from this quarter, or whether he was sufficiently provided for, or was himself capable of providing it, I never found out since on that matter he observed a notable silence, notwithstanding excellent collaboration with us. It was, however, plainly evident that he had access to a large reserve of funds. My own situation was that I had to be content with an initial capital of a couple of hundred thousand *pengö*, half of which derived from Jewish and half from Christian sources, fortunately with no strings attached regarding the proportions in which it was to be distributed. That was purely a matter for my own discretion.

Under such circumstances, however, our administration could clearly not be burdened by a larger outlay of expenses than what was absolutely essential. Our first office was provided free of charge by the Hungarian Red Cross, and in step with the growth in activity there were almost daily offers of suitable new premises. A satisfactory 'Aryan' workforce was of course not freely available since the removal of Jews from commercial life had led to almost every Christian office worker capable of typing or composing a passable letter being taken on to replace them. Unpaid Jewish staff, on the other hand, were available in unlimited quantities, and this was the course we took – the only one feasible – in spite of the risks that it involved.

There was, it is true, one other resource, although a rather meagre one. Before everything had been settled, I had already requested from the Central Committee in Stockholm two Swedish female assistants for whom I entertained the very best of hopes: one was Asta Nilsson, who following the end of the First World War had been head of the Swedish children's nursery unit in Budapest, while the other was Malla Granath, who in a spirit of incredible self-sacrifice and courage had succoured the persecuted German Jews in Vienna, and who was seen by them as a true guardian angel. At the same time I had asked for two female office assistants, with a good knowledge of German and each equipped with a reliable Halda typewriter.

If these various requests had been met, our work would have been considerably easier to carry out, and would have gained authority in the eyes of the Hungarian powers-that-were. Nothing much was achieved, however, following the usual exchange of correspondence, except that Ms Nilsson finally arrived late in the summer and took up her position as head of our orphanage department. The Central Committee assumed responsibility for her expenses in Sweden during her absence, while I was to provide for living expenses in Budapest – this made her something of a paid assistant to me, which should be borne in mind in the light of subsequent events. Malla Granath was said not to be available; nobody else arrived in her place, and the typists were never heard from.

From a Hungarian point of view our organisation must have seemed a trifle odd as our Swedish Red Cross was represented by a single delegate and his wife (no-one else within the Swedish community was willing to give up their time) who were surrounded on all sides by Jews, a not altogether welcome situation. Matters were not improved by the fact that it was easy to confuse our activity, geared towards supplying relief to *all* the needy, with the Wallenberg initiative, linked to the embassy, which was solely concerned with aid for the Jewish population. Some of the hundreds of Jews employed there were the cause of some doubt, and this was true of some of our own colleagues, though most were exceptional workers.

In accordance with the programme approved by the Swedish government and seconded by the Hungarian Regent, our task was to assist *all* people in distress, giving priority to unprovided-for women and children, the elderly and the sick; in addition, and not least, those without shelter who had been bombed out and lost all their property, or who in the course of the war had been forced to flee from their home towns outside or inside the borders of Hungary.

At this time there still existed in the provinces a more than adequate supply of food at reasonable prices, and if we had only had the necessary money and transport, we could have acquired pretty well unlimited quantities. Moreover, in many places we were promised the surplus production of a number of farms of varying sizes, either free of charge or at much reduced rates, on condition that we provided the transport. Elsewhere premises were offered us which included holiday and convalescent homes not being used owing to the prevailing circumstances, and where we would have been able to accommodate children and the elderly; similarly, accommodation was offered for the shelter and feeding of refugees who were streaming along the country roads in steadily increasing numbers as the front drew nearer and nearer.

In the capital, too, we were offered houses or flats for our possible needs on a daily basis, as well as voluntary work in health care and office duties. It might well have been an easy matter for us to imagine that our activities had won surprisingly wide recognition in a remarkably short time if a sober consideration of the situation had not told us that behind all this kindness lay a good deal of self-interest – people were eager to assure themselves of the protection of life and property that a connection with the Swedish Red Cross might bring either in the present or in times to come. In many of the cases – in far too many, said our minister – we accepted, partly because the current need rapidly grew, and partly to gain access to reserves should they be needed. If we had only had sufficient suitable staff, more vehicles than those at our disposal, and more abundant means for the purchase of the all-too-expensive petrol, there is no doubt that much more could have been achieved than actually was. We must of course disclaim any responsibility where deference to our emblems and our hire contracts was concerned, but the fact remains that for a long time we had no reason to complain of any lack of respect for them. What troubled us most was that each new agreement usually required a trip for the inspection of the data and information we had submitted, and for the assessment of the suitability of the premises we wished to use and the persons we wished to employ. For these purposes we seldom had time or the staff or even sufficient transport. In the end, certainly, we did have, formally, a dozen vehicles at our command, but the reality was that they were often somewhere else when they were most needed, or they were in a state of disrepair. For example, they all had incredibly worn out but irreplaceable rubber tyres.

Simultaneously, both the number and the range of our tasks increased like wildfire. The first office quickly became unsuitable partly owing to the two small rooms being overcrowded and partly because half the courtyard of the Hungarian Red Cross swiftly overflowed with people waiting for assistance, while the air-raid shelter filled to capacity when the alarm sounded with annoying regularity. On such occasions I usually seized the opportunity to dash through the empty streets in my little sports car and take care of any outstanding business in the form of visits and meetings. Admittedly it was strictly forbidden to be out while the alarm had sounded, and there was a high risk of incurring prosecution and a fine, but on the other hand you could get to where you wanted to go twice as fast or even faster, and I took advantage of this. At 60kph you were quite safe from being apprehended, and the Red Cross and Corps Diplomatique markings on our vehicles obviously were a help so no unpleasantness occurred.

Gradually our work had reached such proportions that people applying for relief were streaming in in their thousands, and the national Red Cross organisation, which of course answered to the Hungarian Ministry of War, was forced to ask us to find other premises in order to avoid everything ending in a total collapse. No harm was done, however. On the contrary, we were able to select some of the premises we had been offered and settle in at our leisure. We had soon acquired a dozen or so houses and flats in different parts of the city for our office requirements; added to these was the large number of places already established and intended to house juveniles.

Jokingly we were beginning to be called the city's biggest house-owner, and our ambassador, who was fretting over what he referred to as an 'inflation of locations', put up more and more resistance whenever I asked him to put his signature on an acquisition request. I did, however, get my way for the most part by never in principle saying no when he asked us to take care of people who were literally assailing him with demands to be given a hiding place in the embassy. Nonetheless, it became something of a sacrifice in time, effort and fuel, which otherwise could have been put to better use for more general and less personal purposes. The natural consequence was that I had scarcely any time left for the necessary inspection of operations in our various departments. For some time to come I enjoyed the help of no more than a *single* competent assistant for these tasks, namely my tireless, obliging, smart and clever wife, and there was never sufficient time to check all the areas required. It was difficult to demand of colleagues who were unpaid and largely inexperienced a devotion to a task I had myself undertaken to perform, a devotion without which a proper execution of the work in hand was impossible.

Now perhaps is the time to give a detailed account of all we were up to; in other words, a general survey of the various branches of our activity. Our new central office was set up in Count Andrássy's private mansion, close to the Italian embassy, which after the First World War had accommodated a Swiss Red Cross office. It had thus a certain tradition behind it, and constituted in itself something of a minor government department. It was headed by our so-called general secretary, who stubbornly hung on to this rather fancy title and who doubtless was a very competent – perhaps overly competent – man. He possessed a large number of ideas, and was blessed with the capacity and the shrewdness to carry them through, either with or against my own wishes and knowledge.

He settled himself comfortably into four large, beautiful rooms with some thirty fellow-workers who had been directly employed, and with goodness knows how many more on the periphery. There were special departments for all necessary activities – cash desk, accounting and correspondence, an office for legal matters such as the drawing-up of formal hire contracts, tenancy agreements and petitions, another for technical details involving our premises, its fittings and the storage of food, a transport section in charge of the dozen or so vehicles we had at our disposal together with the acquisition of fuel, a co-operative providing food to the needy, and a committee which made a preliminary scrutiny of the applications for our 'letters of protection'.

Quite possibly all of this was both useful and necessary; whatever the case, endless quantities of paper and printed material were produced, and flocks of visitors were received, their business seen to by him often independently of me as I was usually busy negotiating with the authorities, or with people who absolutely insisted on going straight to the Red Cross delegate with their problems and their propositions. Additionally, I had to inspect, in as far as it was possible, the various branches of our organisation and the places where it was carried out, as well as plan operations for the coming winter.

The secretary purchased cows and horses, at inexpensive prices or as good as, obtained fodder for them, made deals for delivery from the countryside, concluded agreements for the acquisition of a couple of hospitals, negotiated the transfer to the Swedish Red Cross of the lovely Margaret Island on the Danube in its entirety – in brief, he carried out a magnificent, wide-ranging job, which I should have shouldered had I found the time for it. He properly speaking had only one single fault, which unfortunately was a rather important one – he was not entirely reliable either in word or action! Unfortunately, this never really became obvious until after utter confusion engulfed the country around the turn of the year. As luck would have it, though, he had a much more reliable deputy, who the following year was to become his successor in the job.

One of our more important fields of work, in accordance with the programme that had been set out, concerned orphanages. Pending the arrival of the assistant we had been promised from Sweden, we had appointed a special committee with a secretariat. We had made preparations for the acquisition of beds and bedding, and registered a list of proposed premises. A number of transactions were based on a monthly fee for each child of 240–300 *pengö* (equivalent to 2.5–3€ in today's money), payable either in money or in food. The orphanages were to receive these fees via our cashier's department, which was also responsible for the maintenance of people without means; if there were relatives who were fairly well-off, a similar fee would be requested from them, and we were always grateful when the cost of one or more poor children was met by those who volunteered to help us. Our outlay was thus reduced, and at this time there were still quite a few people who gladly offered their services in exchange for their children benefiting from the kindly treatment and protection of the Red Cross.

Preparations had reached an advanced stage when the Swedish head of department, Ms Asta Nilsson, finally arrived, and with a certain air of solemnity and decked out in her various badges of rank was presented to her colleagues. Her job description entailed taking charge of all activities concerning the children in accordance with the financial principles previously mentioned, inspecting and assessing such premises as had already been offered to us or which were later proposed, concluding the necessary agreements, receiving people who were applying for relief, and once a week inspecting the new homes which had been approved. To this end she was given full access to my own official car with the invaluable CD plates attached together with one of the city's most capable women chauffeurs, Countess Berta Berg, at the wheel. Offices were available in the centre of town – it was only a single room, but could be exchanged for something larger at any time, though less conveniently situated. Her living accommodation was a house belonging to Budapest's leading hospital surgeon, Professor Adam, who partly had us to thank for rescuing him from the clutches of the Germans after he had been imprisoned owing to his Jewish descent and liberal turn of mind.

After Ms Nilsson had had a few days' rest at the first-class Palatinus Hotel on the lovely Margaret Island and I had catered for her immediate needs, with boundless confidence the children's department was left in her experienced hands. So far so good, and when I later visited the premises to see how things were getting along with the staff I had employed, and which I promised to replace if necessary, she appeared to be totally satisfied. For my part I was fully content with the way work was proceeding. Money was flowing in for the children's accommodation in ample quantities. Our estimate that the children's department could more or less pay for itself seemed to be holding good.

Nevertheless, it soon turned out that Ms Nilsson was not happy with her living accommodation, and when she was offered something else she declined. Neither the car nor the chauffeur suited her. When I referred her to our cashier's office through which all payments and disbursements passed and were recorded, so that she could apply there for further compensation for her living costs, she claimed that for the moment she had no special needs. A little while later it turned out that none of the funds being paid in reached the central office – the children's department was holding on to the money and looking after its own economy. New staff was being taken on without my even being consulted. My hands full with other work, and accustomed to coaxing people into doing things by gentle means as far as possible, I refrained for the time being from taking any steps – save in one exceptional case. Another of my colleagues, the general secretary of the Protestant Church, the Reverend Vargha, had put his own orphanages and nursing homes at our disposal in exchange for being able to establish his own church charity organisation within the framework of the Swedish Red Cross and thus benefit from the protection offered by our emblem. One day he asked me whether it was really true that we only took an interest in Jewish children. I wondered how he could arrive at such a thought, and he said he had heard this from one of the new members of the staff recently taken on by Ms Nilsson. I didn't beat about the bush and had the man dismissed immediately. This did not exactly clear the air between me and my departmental head, and relations steadily cooled and were finally broken off. More of this, however, later. We had other tasks to occupy our minds, more important than disputes over organisational matters.

One of our main duties – and as it later turned out the most important one of all – was arranging to the best of our ability shelter and protection for Jews who had still not been deported, and who were beginning literally to lay siege to both Wallenberg's and our own premises. They had been seized by what I judge to be a fully justified terror of being carted away, tortured and finally murdered, and they were now seeking our help to rid themselves of this threat and a subsequent horrific fate. The task lay primarily with the Wallenberg initiative, whose chief objective was to evacuate to Sweden Jews who had close relatives in our country, or who had strong business ties with Sweden. The rest, lacking such connections and thereby not qualifying, immediately looked to us at the Red Cross.

How could we help them? How could we be of assistance to people who appeared to be really in need of aid? We gradually arrived at the notion of creating a kind of 'letter of protection' or identity card more or less in the form of the famous 'Nansen passports' from the period following the end of the First World War. Apart from a photograph and the usual personal details, they would include a humble, respectful request to whatever authorities it might concern to provide the holder with protection and assistance whenever required. In point of fact this was something of a bluff, but since we were not *demanding* anything particular for our *protégés*, just making a polite request – for what it was worth – we felt we were reasonably safe and had nothing to fear. The same idea had occurred to Wallenberg, who issued so-called 'protective passports' on behalf of the Swedish embassy, and which could claim official recognition. Both types of document were given due consideration, however, and in the course of time came to play a major role in saving the lives of thousands of people.

Our small 'letters of protection' resembling passports (they were produced in two formats, one for adults and one for orphaned children) were initially intended for the use of our own colleagues in providing them and their families with a certain sense of security. This applied equally to the children under twelve we had taken care of, and to those people whose rescue we were especially concerned about for cultural and other reasons. Selection was the responsibility of my extremely able wife as manager of what we called our Shelter and Protection department. On the basis of reports and recommendations from our central office, her section provided final scrutiny, issuing the eagerly-awaited documents to the best of their ability and in all good conscience.

At this time we were living with the illusion that our operations in rescuing Jewish citizens would not be a long-enduring affair, nor would it need to be very comprehensive, enabling us to shift our attention to a larger and more general issue: alleviating the hunger and distress which we had no doubt would be afflicting a large part of the population by late autumn. This illusion derived essentially from the determined intervention by the State Regent (more of this in a later chapter) soon after the Swedish King's telegram pleading for a charitable approach towards those being persecuted. This telegram had probably provided Admiral Horthy with the moral strength to act, and it was clear that the general mood of the country had also begun to react against the brutal operations which were now taking place (as far as they could be ascertained), and this was plainly evident even in circles where a friendly attitude towards the Jews could hardly be expected. The State Regent took the matter into his own hands, and on a certain day in July issued the order to stop any further deportations. Those Jews who still remained, mainly in the capital and its immediate vicinity, were no longer under threat. On the other hand, however, relatives and friends of the hundreds of thousands already deported were extremely anxious about what was happening to them in Germany, Austria and the Polish General Government. We were overwhelmed with pleas to investigate.

This gave rise to the opening of a new branch of activity, which naturally aroused a good deal of interest. As soon as the word got around that you could send in queries to the Swedish

Red Cross, letters began to stream in in their thousands. We had to set up a special office with fifty or so colleagues distributing forms to fill in giving details of name and address, date of deportation, etc. Every day some 100 letters arrived through the post, the details of which were registered on index cards. Similar information was recorded on the spot when visitors came and requested help. After only a few weeks we had 60,000 names registered. A postcard was assigned to each letter with a reply stating that we had received the enquiry and would be doing our best to acquire the information, which would then be passed on to the person or persons requesting it.

This office was installed on the ground floor of a large, pleasant villa with a delightful garden which belonged to one of the city's best-known physicians. There was a contract between him and our embassy to the effect that he was guaranteed extraterritorial protection and a number of other privileges, while his son, a high-ranking official at the Foreign Ministry, was very much devoted to us. Nevertheless, the family became exceedingly anxious as every day Jews in their hundreds began to stream in, whereupon we were obliged to move the office to an even more exclusive villa, this one, too, situated in Buda and surrounded by some exquisitely beautiful parkland, reminiscent I thought of parts of Italy. The owner was a charming member of the upper echelons of the country's aristocracy, an important man in Hungarian industry, and he did us some very large favours.

This department was headed by a couple of foreign gentlemen who received a salary in the normal way. One was a Russian who had married in Belgium and become a Belgian citizen – Count M. Kutusov-Tolstoy. We had rescued him and his wife from an extremely dangerous situation and introduced them to the embassy as suitable persons to care for the 200 or so Russian prisoners-of-war in concentration camps – Sweden had taken upon itself the responsibility of protecting the Soviet Union's interests and supervising the treatment of its citizens. Tolstoy had discharged his duties honourably and left the post, after our military attaché had arrived from Rome and considered the job fell within his responsibility. He paid a couple of visits to the internment camp, and apart from us having supplied the gifts he took with him to the camp, the business now lay outside our sphere of interest – I, for instance, didn't even find an opportunity to visit the camp. The Russians later maintained that in this matter at least we had performed a poor job of safeguarding the interests of Soviet citizens.

The Tolstoy couple now took over our office of investigation and enquiry with the assistance of an excellent English colleague, John Dickinson. All three performed their tasks with zeal and precision – as far as the routine job of registration was concerned. My aim, of course, was not to stop at this introductory stage, a registration process which was no more than a mere formality. My object was to set to work at the real task in hand after the enquiries were no longer coming in: to obtain the information that had been requested. My manager, however, refused point-blank to co-operate – he quite simply believed it was impossible, and he could not be brought to realise that if we did not go further the entire mission was pointless. Or else his pessimistic turn of mind had tired him out; whatever the case, he departed for other duties and left me in the lurch.

The matter was not, admittedly, an easy one to tackle, but for one thing I counted on an accommodating approach on the part of the Hungarian transport authorities, with whom I had the best of relations. For another, I sensed that as the war appeared to be turning against the Germans, their attitudes would soften, and in a few cases at least it might be possible to glean some information on the Jewish workforce being employed in the German labour camps. In the absence of any other person suitable to lead operations at this 'investigation and enquiry' department, we were forced to close it down. Our final act of salvation came during the imminent Arrow Cross regime when we were able to rescue the large file of names, etc., and despatch them to the Swedish embassy away from the enemy's eyes. There might otherwise have been dire consequences for all those who had sent in queries and requests.

A similar fate was shared by another branch of our organisation. The difference was that we were treading a path in the opposite direction in this case – we first searched for missing persons, the aim then being to invite the general public to make their enquiries. It was commonly known that, following the massive defeat at Voronjesj west of the upper reaches of the Danube, tens of thousands of Hungarians were prisoners-of-war of the Russians; it was estimated that about 60,000 men were involved, and that about 20,000 had been killed on the battlefield. Concerning the dead, to some extent their next-of-kin at least could be informed, but nobody could say anything about the fate of the three times as many missing. Naturally their nearest and dearest were suffering dire anxiety wondering about them. The queries and questions we put to the Russians received little response, apart from a very few cases where towards the spring of 1942 the International Red Cross in Geneva was given a certain amount of information.

Nonetheless, we began to notice that the Russian radio service was broadcasting details of names, year of birth and home town of Hungarian soldiers in prisoner-of-war camps. We immediately set up a monitoring station in which a couple of young officers together with their typists noted down names and pertinent data every day. After a few weeks the numbers in our card index had grown to some 1,500 – admittedly only a small fraction of those missing, but still perhaps sufficient numbers to warrant inviting the general public to ask whether among our names and locations a relative was registered as alive in a Russian prisoner-of-war camp. The scheme also included a petition to the Russians for a written list of those names that had been broadcast on the radio *before* we had got started on our work – such lists must have existed in the files of the Russian radio service, and once they had been announced they were obviously no longer a secret. We were hoping to return the favour for the Russians by handing over similar details concerning the relatively few Russian prisoners-of-war in Hungary. Properly speaking, this was the responsibility of the Swedish embassy, already charged with looking after Russian interests in Hungary. In the prevailing circumstances the Red Cross was hardly in a position to take any initiatives, at least as long as these matters lay in the hands of the Swedish military attaché.

To tell the truth, we were equally unqualified to deal with the Hungarian prisoners-of-war. Fortunately, though, it was Bulgaria which attended to Hungarian interests in Russia, and its embassy in Budapest was more than happy to accept our help. In order to satisfy every formal demand, negotiations were opened with this embassy, both verbal and in writing, with the purpose of proceeding in such a way that it was we who did the spadework and the Bulgarians who received the credit – an arrangement which fully satisfied both parties!

The fact that both of these initiatives came to a sorry end was none of our fault but was due to the unhappy course of events during the last three months of the year. For example, fearful that the Arrow Cross might ransack our building, one of our female colleagues thought it was her duty to burn all the files we had spent weeks compiling!

Among a series of activities we organised, mention may be made of the care and shelter of the many elderly people in distressed circumstances. Under the leadership of a Catholic priest (who also happened to be a PhD, and quite an adventurous fellow into the bargain!) and the widow of a Hungarian professor of Belgian extraction, strongly recommended by our embassy (two highly respected Aryan workmates, you would have thought) a new office was opened to undertake the administration of a number of apartments that had been offered to us. For various reasons these were not suitable for housing orphans but could be comfortably adapted for elderly people in need of shelter and care. A self-confident mood accompanied the initial stages of work, and the paperwork was handled with all due attention. One advantage was that Red Cross headquarters were not required to spend any extra money: it was unpaid work, as the two of them declared they were capable of depending on their own resources to cover all material needs. In the beginning the organisation created a distinctly positive impression, and much good was indeed done – at different times we had as many as fifteen to twenty old people's homes operating in various parts of the city. Proper inspection of the work in hand was seldom possible, however, owing to my wife's and my own heavy workload and busy schedule – we could only regret the fact that the lack of the *Swedish* work force we had requested led to a whole range of insuperable difficulties.

It was not long, however, before the two leaders were at loggerheads, whereupon our energetic but somewhat imperious lady moved her work and her office to the other side of the river, the Buda side, together with the smart motor-car that the Red Cross had been provided with, but which she swiftly snatched away from under our very eyes. When later on in the year the Danube bridges were damaged and collapsed and the battle for Buda raged at its fiercest, it was impossible for us to carry out any inspections and the professor's widow disappeared from our horizon. The learned doctor/priest vanished into thin air, too: we don't know when or where to. Both of them appear to have been looking after their own interests fairly comfortably rather than those of the people they had undertaken to help – a further example of the difficulties we were up against in maintaining an absolutely selfless attitude now that we were without any Swedish colleagues with that sense of social responsibility for relief work which back in Sweden was something of an indisputable norm.

Much more successful, however, was the collaboration we enjoyed with the Catholic and Protestant churches. We reached an exceptional understanding with both the nuns and the monks who stood under the protection and care – well-meaning but unfortunately not always efficient – of the apostolic delegate. We maintained a steady and mutually advantageous relationship with a large Jesuit monastery under the leadership of Father J. Raile, and with a smaller one, the French Frères de Marie, whose liaison officer, so to speak, was Frère Albert. To an even greater extent we were served by a number of convents, the principal among which were the *Szent*

Sziv (Sacré Coeur) and the Carmelite and Dominican institutions. Most important of all, however, was the work we shared with the so-called 'Social Sisters', a kind of Catholic welfare association whose head, Sister Margit Schlachta, was one of the most gifted women, in heart, mind and courage, I have ever been acquainted with; in the difficult times to come her institute, with its broad range of activities, would prove to be of the most vital importance for our efforts in rescuing human lives under threat of being snuffed out.

These institutions could always guarantee us a safe and secure home for children and the elderly alike – and even entire families – in addition to the departments we had mentioned earlier which dealt with this sort of activity. In this context I cannot fail to make special mention of the absolutely invaluable support given by my wife, devoted as she was to all that the Red Cross stood for. In this she enjoyed the help of a few self-sacrificing individuals, faithful Christians mostly of Jewish extraction. They managed to establish such connections, keeping them going right until the very end despite their lives being in constant danger. We were able to shelter a large number of men and women of all ages regardless of race or faith.

Our Protestant relief work office was supported by representatives of the Lutheran and the Reformed Churches as well as a number of other denominations. I managed to acquire for them Swedish embassy signposts and notices in Hungarian, German and Russian which served as a protection. The managing body was headed by Baron Radvanszky, chairman of the Lutheran church assembly and its exceptionally capable general secretary, the Reverend Vargha. They both performed some extremely important work for us, at no cost, worthy of the highest praise; they deserve all the support and assistance our own church can give them in the future. All that was required on our part in exchange for this blessing was to fit the work done within the framework of Red Cross operations in order for them to enjoy the benefit of our name and possible intervention on their behalf. This was a distinct advantage for us in that it helped to dispel the misrepresentation that our operations, like the Wallenberg initiative, only involved the rescue of persecuted Jews.

This erroneous interpretation of our respective missions was prevalent during the opening stages when these people were exposed to the greatest dangers. For this reason a natural bond of collaboration existed between our two organisations. Among other considerations we shared the common interest in getting hundreds of orphaned Jewish children over to Sweden where the Jewish communities in Stockholm and Göteborg had offered them a safe haven – it was to be a temporary measure, at least until the peace we all yearned for had broken out, so to speak. It also concerned some hundreds of adults with family or business connections in our country, who would thus not represent an added burden to the state authorities and welfare institutions.

Our own good relations with the Ministry of Transport and the Railway Board had resulted in an entire train being made available ready to leave at a moment's notice for Sassnitz on the northern coast of Germany and operate a shuttle service between Budapest and the Swedish ferry line under the control of Hungarian transport officials. All that had to be done, as it were, was press a button to get the ball rolling. Everything depended, however, on the Germans granting a transit permit. Not even Raoul Wallenberg, with his diplomatic status, his abundant supply of money and his incredible energy and enthusiasm managed to get any further than the German embassy accepting up to 300 provisional Swedish passports for Hungarian Jews pending a final decision. Personally I would have preferred to have engaged certain influential people in Sweden to put pressure on the German government, but my request probably never reached its destination. In the end the German decision was merely that visas would certainly be stamped on condition that the Hungarian government agreed to a German counter-claim: the release of a further 300,000 Jews for forced labour in Germany! Quite naturally we refused to co-operate with this. If the Sztójay regime, from the time of the March coup, had still been in power, it is quite possible that this weirdly uneven horse-trading principle would have been gladly accepted. It would have meant almost all remaining Jews being got rid of, while at the same time neutral Sweden's request was being met. In the meantime something had happened which perhaps it is convenient to summarise under the following heading.

INTERMEZZO: Pending . . .

WHEN the Regent issued the order to halt deportations on Saturday 18 July 1944, it was truly the very last moment for the Jewish population in Budapest – practically every single Jew from the provinces, as far as could be gathered, had already been hauled away to Germany or Poland, performing slave labour in the camps or facing extermination in the gas chambers. It's a safe bet that over half a million people had fallen foul of this horrendous treatment, and the remaining few were but a hair's breadth from sharing a similar fate. There is little doubt that King Gustav's telegram was instrumental in Horthy's decision to intervene, a decision based in part on the conviction that the Germans had lost the war; the only way to safeguard Hungary's future was the country shaking off its dependence on the Axis powers while the going was good.

It was of course a risky venture since the country was still surrounded on all sides by German armies, among which a number of Hungarian divisions were embedded. The move towards greater independence could not be made all at once; they had to go forward step by political step. The first of these steps was the establishment of a new legally-appointed government. Whether Sztójay's cabinet offered its resignation following pressure from the head of state himself, or was a result of German manoeuvres which would have him go the whole hog and then become harmless – these questions may be left unanswered for the moment. We can, in any case, be sure that the newly-appointed government under General Lakatos broadly measured up to Horthy's intentions as well as the range of policies he would be likely to embrace in the future. The new list of ministers did not include a single person who could be considered as a particularly firm friend of Germany; a couple of the members of the government were known as being staunch Hungarian patriots owing unbending allegiance to the Regent, something which was definitely not true of the people he had had forced upon him at the time of the March coup.

There can be no doubt that Admiral Horthy had already realised at a much earlier stage that his country was slipping into an extremely dangerous situation in which its interests were being bound up with those of the Axis powers. On a number of occasions he had done what he could to put a brake on this progress towards what sooner or later would be ruin. The power of a constitutional head of state is very limited, however, and he is generally, as we know, dependent on a government which enjoys a parliamentary majority. He must now have found the situation such that Hungary needed to try and ease itself out of a lost cause. He had already intimated to me, in a confidential conversation we had had quite some time before Hungary's forced entry into the war alongside Germany, his personal view that victory – just as in the previous World War – would ultimately fall to whoever gained the upper hand at sea and in the air. At this point in time it was becoming more and more obvious that the Allies were becoming ever more dominant. It was from this perspective that Horthy now chose his new council of ministers.

The first important measure taken by the new Minister of the Interior was to give the two bloody-handed Permanent Secretaries at the Interior Ministry, Baky and Endre, the sack. We greeted this turn of events with a deep sigh of relief, and we sincerely believed that the uneven struggle to rescue the victims of persecution was now happily over. Admittedly, the strict laws controlling the Jewish population had not formally been rescinded, but on the other hand there was now hardly any danger to their lives. Very soon, too, we were to know that the government had clearly and firmly rejected the German demand for Hungary to release another 300,000 Jews for deportation to labour camps. These unhappy people could renew their trust in being left in peace, and when called up for national service rest assured that they would be doing it in normal, decent circumstances within the country. The transfer to Sweden of the relatively few people who had obtained 'protective passports' or 'protective letters of documentation' was no longer on the cards, while Wallenberg was seriously considering returning home as his real mission could be regarded as completed. He decided, however, to remain for the time being – to the good fortune, as it turned out, for many thousands who without his unremitting zeal would have been lost for all time. He extended his operations and gave them the title 'The Royal Swedish Embassy Humanitarian Action'.

As far as my wife and I were concerned, we had no intention of leaving the country and abandoning our work. Of course it did not exclusively embrace the rescue of the Jewish population, even if it was this task which from the start had led to our intervention and started the Swedish Red Cross operation. This branch of activity merely constituted one part of what we hoped and intended to achieve. If it was not now so essential, so much the better, and we would be able to devote our attention and efforts to many other areas of need: the homeless, the bombed-out, the injured and refugees, the elderly, single women and orphans – all those, in short, we could reach and who were threatened by a perilous winter that soon would be upon us as the war continued. In this connection we were painfully reminded of the enormous store of food which we had had access to as late as in June but which eluded us simply because in a certain quarter it had been decided not to invest in a series of exchanges of telegrams owing to the uncertainty of a successful outcome. As often is the case, the official air of pessimism resulted in an impediment for those who had faith in the possibility of success, and who were doing their utmost to overcome every hindrance, even though the final goal may never be attained.

The donations we received from Hungarian sources had nevertheless proved to be sufficient to cover costs so far, but in no way could they enable us make it through the winter. I therefore applied to the Central Committee of the Swedish Red Cross for an advance of the 50,000 Swedish crowns (half a million *pengö*) which was said to have been put aside for relief work in Hungary. I got an affirmative response 'if the sum is necessary and transfer of the money could be carried out'. There was little doubt of its necessity, and as for transfers of funds, they took place all the time both then and later. I forwarded my thanks for the promise I had received but requested a slight postponement to the transfer since we still had the financial means to cover a further two months. Everything pointed to a drop in the value of the *pengö* if the transfer was made now. It was not until later in the autumn that we agreed with Wallenberg to telegraph home for remittance of the money. Whether this was done or not I never found out, but whatever the case we never obtained a single penny, either then or later, from Sweden.

In the meantime, the fighting was getting ever closer, and there was an increasing risk that the coming winter would see a situation of dire need and want. In the course of a rather long trip by car to the south in order to set up a couple of orphanages in the countryside and arrange for substantial deliveries of food from a large estate in southern Hungary, I found myself at a spot that was so close to the front line that the sound of artillery accompanied our midday meal. The Hungarian army's Red Cross vehicles were bringing scores of blood-soaked injured soldiers to the ground floor of the mansion which had been converted into a field hospital, and it was by the skin of our teeth that we managed to return in time to evade the ever more rapidly advancing Russian steamroller.

Agreements had already been reached with a couple of other estate owners along the same route for meals to be provided to the destitute refugees fleeing from the east and who were already choking the country roads, as well as for temporary homes to be set up for the poor children abandoned along the way. We were later happy to be able to confirm that the advancing Russian troops – at least for some time to come – fully respected our notices and placards indicating that this or that place was being used by the Swedish Red Cross. If only we had had enough time, and had more manpower and fuel been available, much more could undoubtedly have been done for these unfortunate people than what our modest capacity allowed. There was a lot we missed simply because time was so short, and because the fuel we needed just couldn't be obtained for trips to more distant areas of the country.

One example should suffice to serve as an illustration. Through the initiative of the head of our embassy, I had visited former Prime Minister Kállay who at the time of the March coup had managed to claim asylum in the Turkish embassy, where, fairly safe from any attack on his person, he lived together with his charming wife while one of their sons had found shelter in one of the monasteries that was working with us. We leased his estate, situated in the eastern part of the country, and a legal contract was drawn up leaving its entire administration and gross production (excluding taxes and salaries) in our hands. Yet before we had had time to put the signs and placards announcing our presence in place, and before a representative could enter the contract in the land register, the area was overrun by Russian troops and the estate was now on the other side of the front line. It lay unprotected and was plundered almost to the last item by the marauding gangs which are wont to accompany any invading army.

Similar occurrences were common in other parts of the country, something which left us empty-handed and with a painful feeling of not being able to lend a needed hand when we could have done, as long as we had had sufficient means and manpower. Sweden had only sent us a single office worker instead of the four we had requested, while it proved to be impossible to recruit any of the few members of the Swedish community in Budapest. Those few I might have been able to count on had either gone home and not returned, or had become involved in commercial or other interests. We were quite simply reduced to going about our business with what we had.

Part of this concerned the personal protection afforded by our identity cards, which were now more and more sought after, even by the so-called 'Aryan' members of the community, who believed they might provide some kind of protection against attack when at any moment the capital could become a war zone. We'd been criticised for our bold attitude in issuing our 'letters of protection' without authorisation from home; my response was that the reason we had not requested permission was that I was sure we wouldn't get it!

To be on the safe side, however, we decided to call on the Hungarian authorities and see how they saw the matter – this all the more since some ministry people, officers and members of the police force, were all becoming interested in our documents both for their own sakes and that of their families. Both the Foreign Minister and the Minister of the Interior in the Lakatos government gave us to understand they had no objection but rather instead would be glad to see the operation continue. Again, for safety's sake, I paid a personal visit to the big white chief at the Justice Department, Minister Vladár, showed him our documents and waited for his reaction. He studied the sheets of paper with the closest attention and then turned towards me with these friendly words:

> I have no objections to make, I congratulate you on such a brilliant idea, and I would like to urge you quite simply to continue with the good work. Allow me please to take this opportunity to express my gratitude for all the work you fine Swedish people have done and wish to do to help our unfortunate country; we shall not forget it when once we've got over our present difficulties.

He added the assurance that should we encounter any unforeseen hindrance from the authorities, he was at our disposal at all times. When I in turn made the polite objection that we didn't wish to bother a doubtless extremely busy public servant, and could quite easily approach a suitable departmental head further down the scale, I received a rather ambiguous smile as a reply, and this exhortation: 'Best you come straight to me, to be on the safe side! I'll gladly be of service to you, using all the power my office provides . . . '

Perhaps we should add here – keeping in mind that we are talking about the Hungarian situation – that this was the very first time we had met, and I was not even in a position of authority to deserve such a fine reception; there were only practical reasons and arguments which weighed. I was thus able to inform the rather uneasy head of our embassy of the gist of our conversation – as well as the unconditional approval given by the two other ministers – and assure him that we had the very top people in the Hungarian government on our side in this matter. It only concerned them, to be honest, and no others, since our so-called 'letters of protection' made no claim to official validity. They did, nonetheless, in time offer us a valuable opportunity to save lives, something which during a new phase in the Swedish Red Cross operations in Hungary would become our biggest and most important task due to the momentous course of events.

Meanwhile, two other issues presented themselves which demanded our immediate attention. One concerned setting up first-aid posts for the population at large, particularly following air raids which were increasing by the day. This matter was resolved fairly easily. A number of Jewish doctors who had lost their jobs made themselves available to us. We were provided with premises by friends in different parts of the city without any more ado, and the necessary equipment was acquired at reasonable cost. Together with the city's own facilities, we had seven first-aid posts of our own in operation: not such a bad situation if you take into account our limited resources – one of the posts had eighty fully-equipped beds.

The other issue concerned establishing hospitals and putting them into operation. We came to an agreement with a few hospitals for us to repair their bomb-damaged buildings, which allowed us in return to have a number of beds at our disposal. One hospital belonging to a Reformed foundation, which was unable to run it, was leased to us, and it served us well in the months that followed. Difficulties arose, however, later on as our agreement stipulated that it should be available to Christian patients only – at the start not much notice was taken of race or religion, but when the Arrow Cross regime came to power towards the end of the year the foundation dared not risk any dangerous conflicts.

At the same time we put in an order at a relatively favourable price for a large number of excellent hospital beds made of white enamelled iron which we considered we could afford. A fabulously generous proprietor of a bedding firm made us a present of sorely-needed mattresses, pillows, sheets and pillow-cases. Getting these articles released for our use was not so easy, however, as the army tended to requisition pretty well all such deliveries. Permits had therefore to be sought from the proper authorities and then a licence was granted. This meant applying to the Trade and Industry ministries, inordinately busy as they were with a host of other matters. Thanks to the good reputation which the Swedish Red Cross enjoyed, however, we were generally successful, and found that this reputation opened doors, as it were, for us as long as the legal government remained in power. The various procedures all took their due time, nonetheless, as did the transport to our premises of the articles we had either received as gifts or had ourselves ordered.

None of this would have been possible, however, had we not had access to a special motorised section made up of a dozen or so vehicles mostly supplied by well-wishers. One awkward question was of course the acquisition of petrol and oil, always scarce items. A barrel or two could be obtained as a gift, but as a rule fuel had to be bought at exorbitant prices on the black market. A number of excursions were made to this end by our competent volunteer drivers, among whom were a couple of splendid reserve lieutenants on leave from the army. They often experienced an amusing incident or two out on the roads when, for instance, they met some German military vehicles and in exchange for some small present were able to get hold of cans full of precious fuel, ironically intended for quite different purposes. Without the assistance of this well-organised section we would have lost any number of opportunities of fulfilling our duties. If we had had more money, moreover, we would have been able to purchase a couple of vehicles ourselves to add to my own little Skoda which was exclusively at our disposal, and we would have been in a position to stockpile the petrol we needed. Instead we were reduced to counting every penny when it came to this expensive commodity, and be content with vehicles which were often in use somewhere else. They all suffered from their tyres being worn out and unserviceable, and had to be sent off for repair, which left us at a standstill while a lot that could have been done remained undone.

This was especially true of our relations with the countryside. One of our most important tasks was obtaining sufficient food to meet the coming winter, about which we knew nothing other than it inevitably was going to bring hunger, want and distress – and that is what it brought, to a degree even more appalling than we could have imagined. We had been enjoined by our embassy not to establish connections further outside the capital than 50km. This restriction was, in fact, quite unnecessary since only in exceptional cases did we have access to petrol sufficient for longer trips; but it also put a brake on our activity whenever opportunities arose offering real advantages. We didn't always stick to the letter of the law either, particularly after I had obtained the Kállay estate commission mentioned earlier, which meant travelling over 250km from Budapest. There had been a very good harvest that year, anyway, and food was available in large quantities relatively close to the city.

The connections we established were of a variety of types, and we concluded agreements for the delivery of considerable amounts of food, while setting up orphanages and nursing homes in various places. Contracts were signed, for instance, with a number of interested land owners in a nearby Protestant diocese whereby a hundred or so people employed by us worked as a co-operative providing food to the needy. The farm bailiff of a large estate to the west of the city promised to supply us with the commodities necessary for the very first 'soup kitchen', which was set up by one of our colleagues in collaboration with the city authorities, and which was opened with pomp and ceremony by our ambassador. A prominent farmer of aristocratic stock, chairman of the provincial chamber of agriculture, promised to set up a soup kitchen on his own property for refugees fleeing from the east, and joined our own organisation as head of the section dealing with the purchase, supply and storage of food. A director of the big partially state-run organisation Futura, founded to control all Hungarian corn production for export, approached both the Red Cross and especially our embassy, where the very efficient attaché, Per Anger, outlined plans for ensuring the food requirements of embassy staff and the Swedish community in Budapest for the coming winter. Spacious storage premises were made available, partly for our own benefit and partly for that of the embassy.

At about this time it happened that our acting vice-consul in Zagreb, Yngve Ekmark, who was also attached to the Swedish–Hungarian Match Company, was compelled to leave his post because of the civil conflict in Yugoslavia and return to what had been his proper place of work in Budapest. This seemed to me to be a heaven-sent opportunity to use his first-class financial expertise, as well as his being a worthy successor should anything happen to me. We had been very close friends for a long time, and I was sure I could count on his assistance. The embassy had similar plans, however, and a greater natural claim to him in view of his 'unemployed vice-consul' status. His services were thus divided, and quite naturally our organisation, being the weaker of the two, got the worst of it.

With winter conditions in mind, the size of Red Cross operations had expanded considerably from what had originally been planned, and I was in urgent need of the help of a couple of wise and energetic deputies. A meeting of our departmental heads was called – Asta Nilsson took part as such, though she would later deny such status – and it was decided that I would be assisted by a head of an administrative section and a head of a financial section. The first post was occupied by the colleague we referred to earlier, Count Kutusov-Tolstoy, who had made a good job of setting up our archives researching Jewish citizens who had disappeared, but who, as we also remarked, had grown tired of his work. The other position was taken over by Ekmark, who in the event of my possible illness or death would take my place as delegate and run the entire operation.

We had by chance just gained possession of new, spacious and well-situated premises to house my secretariat, a place where the three of us could work together on a daily basis. The arrangement, however, barely lasted a week. I shouldn't blame others, and perhaps the fault was mine. What happened was the following: Tolstoy, who was paid for his job, came into conflict with our unpaid secretary-in-chief, who was in charge of our central office and its many branches, and who was not inclined to accept a situation whereby another person was shoved in between him and the Red Cross delegate. The Count asked to be released from this undertaking so as to devote himself to the soup kitchen – a task he performed quite brilliantly for a time – and later, commissioned by the embassy, he was made head of a hospital annexe for wounded Russian prisoners-of-war. This was an excellent and praise-worthy institution which, unfortunately, during the Arrow Cross period came into conflict with the Hungarian military authorities, went into decline, and finally ceased to exist. As far as Ekmark was concerned, he turned up only once in the office reserved for him at my secretariat. The reason for this was not revealed to me until later. Among other matters he had been occupied on embassy business at the former Finnish embassy, which was now housing a Swedish section while Sweden had been appointed to take charge of Finland's interests. He now appeared to consider it was I who should visit him for our meetings rather than vice versa. He was also upset by the fact that I had taken on some lesser-known but very capable people to acquire food for our operations, which I had done because the embassy channels were strictly speaking only intended to serve Swedish interests.

We enjoyed the great benefit of a close relationship with a large organisation which dealt with the supply of food to the capital, with cold stores and ample warehouse space, much of it filled to capacity. We had reached agreements with this firm which were so much the more important as the enterprise was intimately bound up with the country's biggest bank, and could arrange financial aid and credits from the industrial and banking sectors, among them the Hungarian National Bank. The sum of two million *pengö* was involved, an amount frankly not to be sneezed at in our present position. It had of course been my intention to negotiate these affairs together with Ekmark, but as we never seemed to be both available at the same time, I was forced to take the matter into my own hands.

We were thus in a position to make use of every possibility that presented itself for providing assistance, whatever happened, in the struggle to combat hunger, illness and misery in the difficult winter months before us. The noble farm-bailiff we mentioned earlier helped us link up our operations with those of the embassy led by Ekmark, but essential differences of opinion remained which did not exactly favour further collaboration. I myself was deprived of the opportunity to engage some valuable 'pillars of strength' in a job which was beginning to weigh heavily on my aging shoulders. It would have been so much easier to bear if we had been 'three men in a boat' rather than now when I had to steer my own vessel alone, with my loyal wife as second officer on the bridge!

Nevertheless, we were able to sort things out and gloss over our differences, always an eventuality in any choice of practical working methods. I acquired a couple of splendid

Hungarian colleagues for my secretariat, both ex-departmental heads, one from the Ministry of Culture and the other from the Ministry of Finance. They had had close connections with our country and had visited Sweden several times on official business.

One of them, Dr Géza Paikert, had been an intimate friend of mine for many years. We had often co-operated in efforts to strengthen cultural ties between our two countries, and I had, for one thing, had the pleasure of introducing him to our Minister of Education. During the 'Swedish Days' exhibition in Budapest in 1943 Paikert had performed some invaluable services, as a result of which he had been decorated with the Swedish Royal Order of the Northern Star. At the time of the March coup he had avoided being arrested as an 'adversary of Germany' or even dismissed from his prominent post at the ministry. He was relegated to an unimportant role, however, where he had nothing special to do, and drifted into a kind of permanent leave of absence, which afforded him the opportunity to put himself fully at our disposal.

The other one, Dr István Vásárhelyi, had been commissioned to hold important financial negotiations with foreign countries, and was an eminent specialist in his field as well as an excellent negotiator. Just the same, he was seen by the Sztójay government, sworn allies of the Germans, in a very negative light – he, too, had been pushed aside and put on permanent leave. During the Arrow Cross regime in the final months of the year, both these men feared for their lives yet stood firm side-by-side with us through thick and thin up to the moment they were compelled to go into hiding to avoid being killed. Following the big upheaval in the New Year, Vásárhelyi was restored to the democratic government and held the post of State Secretary and head of several sections within the Ministry of Finance. At the same time he joined our Red Cross committee and performed a number of invaluable services for us.

Our collaboration with the Swedish embassy's financial

division under Ekmark continued satisfactorily for the time being. We managed – at least partly – to get some of our own people to co-operate in stockpiling food, ensuring that warehouses in various localities were kept full stocked, sufficient in any case to meet reasonable demands. If things had gone on undisturbed, both our organisations would have been well-equipped for the task in hand. Fate, however, took a course other than that which our human calculations had envisaged.

The legal government appointed by the Regent at the end of the summer, following his own plans and intentions, appears to have come to the evident conclusion that any continued co-operation with Germany must inevitably lead Hungary to disaster. The mighty neighbour to the west stood more or less alone now in Europe after the fall of Italy, at least as far as the military goal – the submission of an entire continent – was concerned. The vast Russian armies were crushing all in their path as they marched westwards. They had thrown the invaders out of their own country and plunged deep into the territory of their neighbours to the west. Romania yielded to them, and in Hungary they were now in possession of the larger part of the country to the east of the Danube. It seemed to be but a matter of weeks before any resistance would be useless. Some sort of negotiations had probably been initiated by suitable intermediaries during September, and from those quarters that were – or believed themselves to be – involved in the secret goings-on premature rumours were being spread to the general public. Thus one of my staff, for example, came along with the 'absolutely reliable' information to the effect that on the night of 12 September a delegation had travelled to the frontline in the north-east to negotiate a truce; he could even name the general whose task it was supposed to have been!

If the nation had been united, so much would not have been at risk, since both in the east and the south as well as partly in the north the German grip on the country had loosened. Those high-up in the army and in the civil administration, still quite numerous, who had sworn allegiance to Germany and either openly or in secret were members of the Arrow Cross, now had to choose between trying to grab power or having to suffer the consequences of the stand they had taken. A successful coup might in any case gain them a short respite and possibly, if Germany was able to hold the fort, allow them to come up trumps.

Whichever way, it was now a matter of going for the best set of values, for the country's future survival. It would be unjust to deny every single Arrow Cross follower a patriotic spirit, for even among them there were surely many who were driven by ideals and sincere conviction. The terrible, savage turn of events which later led to murderous bands of marauders roaming the streets of the city was undoubtedly not what the leaders at that time had intended. It had its sad psychological explanation partly in the hatred towards the Jews which was widely prevalent, and partly in the dreadful mentality fostered by the war which praised all manner of destruction and devastation, and finally in the absolute lack of competence of those who had been elevated to or had themselves assumed power, for which they were highly unsuited both politically and practically, and in a number of cases morally unfit as well. They were, and they remained, henchmen of the insane Hitler-Himmler regime, but at the same time they were incapable of keeping a tight rein on the riff-raff's murderous instincts.

If a sufficient number of reliable people in leading positions in the army and the civil administration had backed the legal government, the latter might well have found an opportunity at the beginning of October to carry out its ill-concealed plans. Developments might then have taken another path, and this ancient kingdom might have been saved, albeit at the cost of heavy loss of life. But the necessary prerequisites were absent. There was insufficient time to prepare a firm basis for the proper policies to be adopted. The Germans together with the Arrow Cross found out what was being planned through their network of spies and were ready to upset the apple cart. Neither were people loyal to the government ignorant of the planned operations. It was simply a matter of first past the post, of which of the parties could gain the upper hand first. Whether fate had a hand in the affair, or whether it was due to a lack of foresight and skill on the part of those who sat at the helm of state, whatever the case the move made led to the head of state finding his powers severely curtailed.

THE THIRD ACT:

Under the Arrow Cross

I⊤ was Sunday 15 October 1944. I was visiting my wife, whose office at that time was in the huge and exclusive *Szent Sziv* (Sacré Coeur) convent close to the city park. The dear little sisters, headed by their tiny abbess, all skin and bone, Mother Superior Mme Klamperer, a native of Belgium, accompanied by their financial manager, Mother Hildegard, were among our best and most reliable colleagues. Among other things, we ran an orphanage there for little Jewish children, for whom we acquired beds and food, and who were given warm and tender care and schooling as well. There, and at the Dominican nuns' smaller convent, we had at our disposal room for over 250 of our adult *protégés*. We were able to offer space for approximately the same number of people at the Social Sisters' excellent institutions run by Sister Margit Schlachta and Sister Dominica. Finally, there was in this area a hospital which worked alongside us – all in all, it was, so to speak, a tiny Swedish Red Cross corner in the huge expanse of the city of Budapest.

We had attended the day's church service and had lunch in the refectory together with our *protégés* and the principal Sisters. I had walked out into the large garden to take advantage of the calm, sunny autumn weather and its delightful blooms and diaphanous air, the yellowing tree-tops, birdsong and flower-beds not yet beset by frost, while I meditated in splendid isolation over the next set of jobs I would need to get to work on. High brick walls surrounded the vast convent buildings, and an atmosphere of peace and stillness reigned which stood in sharp contrast to our daily hustle and bustle and our growing fears of the perilous winter which was almost upon us.

The big question now was whether the Germans would abandon Budapest and retreat to a new line of defence farther west. In which case the Hungarian capital would avoid being squeezed between two fronts and mercilessly bombarded by incessant air raids and constant shelling. On the other hand, however, it might suffer the miserable fate of so many other beautiful cities. What, one wondered, could our brave little band of workers in the vineyard do against the destruction and havoc caused by the storm of fire among the innocent, suffering civil population? We knew so little, for the daily press kept very quiet about events around us while literally flooding their pages with reports from fronts far away.

I was roused from these reflexions by a shout from my wife who I saw approach me, her eyes shining and arms outstretched.

'What an amazing prophet you've turned out to be!' she exclaimed, and hugged me tight, tears of joy in her voice.

'What's up?' I asked, fully unaware.

'Don't you remember how, more than two years ago, you forecast the end of the war for 15 October 1944, this very day, in fact? And to imagine that at two o'clock, just now, the Regent announced a truce and immediate negotiations with Russia! It's a dream come true – an end to all the bitterness and misery. So we can carry out our work undisturbed to help the needy this coming winter.'

I hardly dared believe her words.

'Come on in,' she said, 'you can hear it for yourself. They're reading out the same announcement all the time so everybody will know. Marvellous, isn't it? We're all overjoyed up there in the house . . . '

It *was* marvellous. Almost inconceivable, despite the rumours that had been circulating recently. The fact that the date coincided with my prophecy was pure chance. My choice of date had come about as a result of a number of obstinate but well-meaning people putting the same old question: 'When d'you think this ghastly war will be over?' There was, however, some kind of logic in my reply. Using a bit of plain common sense and reasoning, late in the summer of 1942 you could scarcely conceive that there could be *more* than another two wartime winters after the Germans' unsuccessful attempts to achieve their most important objectives: the Suez canal and the Caucasian oil fields. The autumn of 1944, if not before, would have to be the moment of peace – the date itself was a mere shot in the dark. Yet now the oddest thing had happened: my prediction, uttered in all earnestness, had hit the mark. My mind boggled, and I couldn't help feeling a bit bumptious; a pity I hadn't had a bet on it – I'd be a rich man today! We certainly could have done with the money then . . . It was a short-lived pleasure, however; there *was* to be a third war winter – the sixth since the outbreak of the war. And in comparison with the hell we were to go through, everything we had had to suffer previously would pale into insignificance.

Already by five o'clock that same afternoon the tune had changed on the radio, so that people not yet in the know were left speechless. A fresh proclamation from the Regent was read out, contradicting the first one. It simply said that the first announcement was the result of an imposture, and that the implacable struggle against Russia would continue with all might and main.

How did matters really stand? Had Admiral Horthy had some sort of seizure while his government had lost their heads? Nobody could explain what had happened. A series of rumours floated around the city, and we all spent a worrisome night. It was not until the following day that things began to make sense: a new *coup d'état* had evidently taken place, a revolution pure and simple, which had deposed the Regent and handed power to his opponents. The move he had tried to make had been countered by another – he fell victim to the coup he had wanted to prevent. He had laid his cards on the table prematurely in the belief that the trumps were his, while in

76

fact what he did was release a mighty storm which got the better of him. His opponent was quicker off the mark, and above all more powerful. The Germans possessed the means of force and had control of the city. All they had to do was press a button for the Arrow Cross to spring into action under the protection of their bayonets. The ensuing explosion shook the state of Hungary to its foundations and brought it to the very brink of ruin.

As the press was of course subjected to the most stringent censorship, and since none of the information we received verbally was fully reliable, it was not easy to obtain a clear picture of what had happened and how it had occurred. Gradually we were able to see the true course of events, however.

On the Sunday morning, the former ambassador, Miklós Horthy – the Regent's only surviving son following the other's death when his plane had crashed near the Russian front a couple of years earlier – was visiting an acquaintance on the Pest side of the river. His car was stopped by German soldiers armed with hand grenades. It was known – evidently via espionage – that the young Horthy had compiled a complete dossier of the brutal incidents which had taken place during the deportations and the Germans were now keen to seize the opportunity to get hold of him. As he stepped out of the car and made for the doorway, a hand grenade was thrown and Horthy fell to the ground, badly wounded in the stomach and chest, after which he was dragged away by the soldiers. Pistol shots were aimed at the car and an accompanying gendarme was hit. The chauffeur drove off at full speed and made for the Palace on the other side of the Danube to seek help – alas, in vain.

This act of aggression towards his own son was the last straw for the aging Horthy. He swiftly summoned his loyal colleagues, and it was decided to take a chance. This was, then, the fundamental reason for issuing the proclamation, which announced a total break in relations with Germany and the initiation of negotiations with the rapidly advancing Russians.

77

The fact that this could be done without consulting Parliament was due to the wide powers which had been earlier granted to the government. Since the present cabinet had unquestionably been appointed in a fully legal fashion – in contrast to the earlier one, where undemocratic pressure had been brought to bear on the Head of State – it was within its rights in deciding to take the most radical political and military measures.

The first proclamation was countersigned by the Chief of the General Staff, General Vörös, and was clearly legally correct. The second proclamation, on the other hand, totally repudiating the first one, lacked a ministerial signature. The conclusion to be drawn was that either the Regent's signature had been forged or Horthy had signed with a gun to his head. Knowing the old admiral's manly disposition and fearless temperament I feel convinced that the first version is the correct one. A third possibility does exist, however, and that would involve him giving way under threat of massacres on the streets of Budapest and the assassination of his more influential colleagues; after all, something similar had taken place on the occasion of the March coup, and might now have been repeated on a larger scale. Yet if this was the reason for his concession – who can sound the depths of a human heart and believe oneself capable of judging a person who has been deprived of the opportunity to describe the motives behind his conduct?

While making the Head of State, in the eyes of the general public, responsible for an act of unprecedented frivolousness with these two contradictory proclamations, the new powers-that-were swiftly proceeded to secure his person. Horthy was imprisoned and shortly afterwards taken by car to Germany, together with his wife, daughter-in-law and grandson, and detained at an unknown location – reported to be somewhere in the neighbourhood of Salzburg. Miklós, his badly injured son, was said to have been interned in Graz. Admiral Horthy disappeared from our history; there were a couple of occasions later in Budapest when he was reported dead, but the latest we have heard is that he had been found by American troops and

ildemar Langlet, chief delegate in Hungary for the Swedish Red Cross (1944–5). Langlet knew the
*untry intimately after living there for many years, and had published a book on his exploits in the 1930s
:ling 1,000km across the country on horseback. His efforts to save those being persecuted in Budapest
.d its surroundings towards the end of the war were started practically from scratch.

A Swedish Red Cross 'letter of protection' popularly known as a 'Langlet passport'.

A page from a 'letter of protection', with Valdemar Langlet's signature.

A Red Cross plaque, with text in Swedish and Hungarian. The protection they offered was highly valued in Budapest.

Elisabeth Bridge, spanning the Danube, was blown up by the Germans.

Kálvin Square in central Budapest at the end of the war.

Valdemar Langlet (right) together with the Legation Secretary Per Anger at the gates of the Swedis Embassy in Budapest.

onsignore Gennaro Verolino, the Papal Nuncio's secretary, who worked closely with Langlet.

Soviet soldiers crossing the Danube and approaching Budapest in December 1944.

Extreme hunger brought many among the inhabitants of the city out on to the streets to take what meat they could scavenge from the corpses of horses.

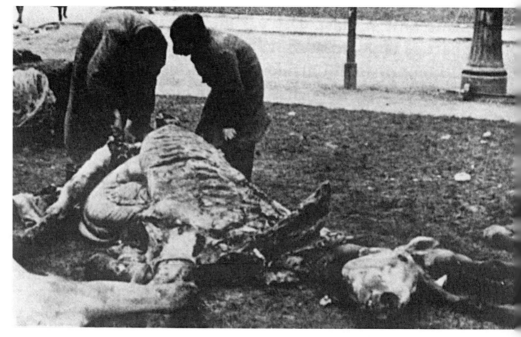

ams, cars and pedestrians were plunged into the icy waters of the Danube when the Margaret Bridge was
:molished by accident. The Germans had mined all the bridges over the river, and intended blowing
em up if they were forced to retreat.

In 1955 the Budapest City Council decided to name a street and a school after Valdemar Langlet. Th
lower picture shows pupils at the school honouring Langlet and his wife at the institution of a scholarsh
fund for students.

taken into safe custody. His son is understood to have recovered from his injuries, and has at present found a safe haven on the island of Capri.

Generally speaking, it is fairly useless discussing after the event what could or should have been done to face up to a situation which in all probability was in the hands of unlucky fate anyway. All the same, it is fairly certain that a series of serious mistakes had been made in the government circles responsible for the lamentable situation which arose on 15 October. More than anything else, an absolute prerequisite for proclaiming the break with Germany should have been making sure support was forthcoming from the army high command – if by no other means, by a number of transfers and/or new appointments to the leading posts. Whatever the case, steps should have been taken to ensure that the garrison, police and gendarmerie would obey orders without question, and that telegraph, postal and radio services were given adequate and reliable protection.

It appears, however, that these were just the steps that were *not* taken. Both the telegraph office and the radio station were immediately stormed, the few guards on patrol were eliminated, and officials loyal to Horthy arrested, apart from those who had managed to flee or go into hiding. Now the coast was clear for a 'news service' which would sow confusion among the authorities and create the impression for the general public that they were living in a madhouse. It might seem the height of irresponsibility to have neglected these apparently self-evident precautions before breaking off relations with a powerful ally and proceeding to negotiate with what until that moment had been an enemy, even though with the conviction that the action would have been welcomed with real joy and satisfaction among the broad masses of the war-weary population, hardly sympathetic to the German cause. Nonetheless, if truth be told there was scarcely time to take the necessary steps; it was said that the government had received a report warning of an imminent coup, which it was *obliged* to nip in the bud. When the young Horthy was then attacked, this was probably seen as a sign that the revolt was at hand, to which it was essential to respond immediately, albeit the necessary precautions for defending the legality of the government were not yet in place.

In other respects the German instigators of the coup, just as on 19 March, enjoyed the advantage of it being a Sunday, when government offices were closed. Any doormen, accustomed to obeying orders and incapable of putting up resistance, would open up for the well-equipped detachments that were sent and which 'in the name of the government' seized control of the buildings. Everything followed a set pattern – the March coup had provided the practice they needed, and the same swift and effective methods were now applied.

On the Monday all of the higher officials loyal to Admiral Horthy were arrested, whether they in all good faith turned up at their places of work or remained at home – a few had the presence of mind to go into hiding or by roundabout ways reach Russian-held territory (among them, the Minister of Defence in what was to be the provisional government later on). Similarly, all known politicians of a leftish inclination were thrown into prison as well as all prominent Jews in the world of business, those who had been unable to save their skins by fleeing the city. A number of those arrested were taken to Gestapo headquarters and the more important cases were transported to Germany; yet others were entrusted to the Hungarian secret police whose chief officer had done a complete turnabout and had placed himself at the disposal of the perpetrators of the coup.

Who were the people who were now going to steer the country? Obviously the Germans stood behind them, but they were of course wise enough not to assume responsibility formally and thereby arouse the Hungarian nation's ill-will more than necessary. The need for a bunch of henchmen was easily satisfied: their front men came quickly to the scene of action. Probably, though, behind the scenes a bitter struggle was going on to gain hold on the reins of power.

A less ill-fated solution, and a more natural one, would have been the appointment of former Prime Minister Imrédy as head of the government. A very ambitious and self-assured individual, a firm friend of Germany and an anti-Semite, he was a leading figure in the parliamentary group which was made up of his own supporters and the Arrow Cross faction. He had the gift of the gab, and had a sound political background and long experience in administration. In addition, he was known for his outstanding financial capabilities, and was looked up to as an honest patriot of impeccable pedigree. Either this one trait was what failed him, or he himself found it unacceptable to come to power by the wrong path. There was probably a good deal of truth in a rumour which claimed that he had actually been urged to take power but had set conditions which the Germans would not accept – but there was no way of checking if this was true.

Another man instead took over, and allowed himself to be appointed using the false signature of the Regent: the former political criminal Major Ferenc Szálasi, a little quisling of a man, but a gifted populist worshipped by his supporters as the principal spokesman of the most aggressive hatred towards Jews. He had managed to achieve what no-one else had succeeded in doing: gather together under one flag the various groups of Hungarian National Socialists, usually warring among themselves, and thus facilitate the formation of a parliamentary block consisting of the Arrow Cross and the bourgeois group on the far right which had united around Imrédy. It was claimed that Szálasi was inspired by idealistic motives and an honest conviction, something which will not be called into question in these pages. There are many such men, however, who are summoned to lead the affairs of a country in perilous times, particularly in world situations which required first-rate statesmen at the head of their nation.

Subsequent to his short period as prime minister in a country without a Head of State, Szálasi began to follow the notorious examples of a *Duce*, a *Führer*, a *Caudillo* and a Quisling, elevating himself by his own accumulation of power to *Nemzetivezetö* – National Leader. As such, he became the last in a series of self-appointed dictators. He can hardly have suspected then that he was going to be the first to fall, as it were the first in a line of dominoes. As a former regimental officer with ambitious dreams, he was similar to Quisling, and had unsuccessfully tried to form a party on the basis of an imported National Socialist model. Like his Norwegian colleague, he had been elevated to his position of authority thanks to violent German power politics. Their end bears a similarity too: defeat, imprisonment, trial and sentence – Szálasi will surely not escape this fate either, unless it has already taken place at the time of writing.[1] Nevertheless, unlike Quisling – whose name has already entered the world's vocabulary spelt with a small letter – Szálasi will not even attain semi-heroic status. He has already been, or soon will be, consigned to the ranks of the eternally forgotten by all who do not have a special interest in the history of Hungary.

The new government's principal tasks were two-fold. Firstly, the country had to be 'purged' of its remaining Jews, now essentially restricted to the capital, in order to provide the German ally with the required amount of slave labour for their war industry. Secondly, too, there was the obligation to help the Germans by making a supreme effort to drive the victorious Russian armoured divisions out of Hungarian territory.

The first task was reasonable and rewarding – the second proved to be unattainable. Blindly trusting in the powerful neighbour's superior war machine, the new people in charge made an enormous error concerning their capacity to bring the Russian steam-roller to a halt and force it back off Hungarian territory. This lack of vision would appear all the more inexplicable in view of the fact that already by the beginning of September both Finland and Romania had been compelled to accept a truce and surrender, not only breaking with

[1] Translator's note: Szálasi was tried by a People's Tribunal in Budapest at the end of the war and sentenced to death for war crimes and high treason. He was hanged in Budapest in 1946.

Germany but also declaring war on their former ally. The Baltic states, moreover, were almost entirely in Russian hands, while General Malinovsky had seized the whole of Sieben-bürgen and large areas of southern Hungary, whereupon from the south and from the east he proceeded to march towards the Hungarian capital. Bulgaria was completely free of Germans and had submitted to Russian control, which gave General Tolbuchin's army free rein to penetrate the south of Hungary west of the Danube and end with a vital pincer movement to capture Budapest.

Whether it was a matter of not *wishing* to comprehend the seriousness of the situation and of an illogical hope of a final German victory, or whether in sheer desperation there was a desire to cause as much damage as possible in the short time remaining, the government apparatus was set in motion with all the forces at its command. Little difficulty was encountered, it seemed, in getting hold of the required number of well-informed people trained in administration who were eager not to miss the boat, so to speak, satisfying the various demands for ministerial posts as well as the vanity and hunger for power of the heads of the different factions. The result was what could be expected. Portfolios were handed out to those who in the vast majority of cases had no idea how to deal with public affairs, and whose merits were totally unknown outside the narrow confines of party circles.

Chosen to be Foreign Minister was a young aristocrat Baron Kemény, formerly an unsuccessful journalist, who just before the coup had occupied a position as an assistant at a small publishing firm in which his literary-minded wife held some shares while also being employed there. Both of them were, in any case, educated, well-mannered people of a friendly disposition. This was far from the case as regards the minister's closest deputy, a highly unpleasant man of the worst Arrow Cross type, who stood in vivid contrast to his predecessor, the ambassador Arnóthy-Jungert. The latter was a trained diplomat, upon whose goodwill towards the Swedish Red Cross we could rely without fail; now, however, he had been detained because a copy of the peace treaty from the end of the First World War had been found on his desk – this was considered proof of his criminal intent to bring to an end the present war!

Among other ministry employees there were a number occupying the same positions as before who had no particular political allegiance, and who for practical reasons were indispensable, and who with dogged resolution were willing to adapt to the changed circumstances. Fortunately for us they included a couple of departmental heads I had had a lot to do with in the course of my work, and whose willingness to help we could still count on, as far as they could without risking to life and limb. Gradually we managed, albeit with some difficulty, to obtain permission for our organisation to continue its work on the basis of the recognition it was had been granted by the Sztóvay regime at the beginning of July. As we had enjoyed a particularly good reputation during the Lakatos regime, this was to be the third Hungarian government to acknowledge our organisation. In time, following an intermezzo of violent persecution during the last days of the Arrow Cross government, we would find favour with a fourth Hungarian government, which has come to power in the current year and at the time of writing is still in office.

The leading post in the cabinet – what we in Sweden would refer to as the prime minister – was also taken over by an educated man who clearly had good intentions towards us. As Szálasi's deputy, this man, whose name was Szöllösi, was said to be a former pharmaceutical chemist from Makó in southern Hungary, a city which by 10 October was already in Malinovsky's hands. His head of cabinet turned out to be an old friend of mine: a charming, skilful and experienced man who had occupied this position of trust through half-a-dozen different governments dating back to Count Teleki's time. On the recommendation of a leading figure in the country's largest banking concern (which we had collaborated with in securing various supplies of food and which had provided us with considerable financial assistance), I was able to take advantage of a happy coincidence and establish a valuable relationship with the newly-appointed head of an extremely influential press department – a very cordial and very intelligent young journalist called Ferenc Fiala. We were subsequently especially grateful to him for much good advice and valuable hints and suggestions which he passed on to us in the utmost confidence. He often went as far as risking life and limb, and personally saved the lives of at least a score of persecuted Jews.

The more moderate group closest to Szálasi included the holder of the Ministry of Justice portfolio. He had apparently risen from humble beginnings, and perhaps it was this fact that induced him to be ready to strike hard whenever the worst elements in the streets wrought havoc. On one occasion he assured me, and pressed the assurance home with the sturdy handshake of a blacksmith (probably his former trade), that as soon as proof could be shown of who the perpetrators of robbery, murder and other violent crimes were, he was prepared to immediately bring into play the entire machinery of a court martial. Unfortunately, it might be pointed out, this never seemed to materialise since men of violence are rarely in the habit of giving their names and addresses so their identity can be established later on!

There were no more than half a dozen such men in the Arrow Cross government, admittedly true friends of Germany and hostile to the Jews, but who wanted to push through their programme while avoiding unnecessary brutality. However, most of the ministers were blind fanatics, among them at least three or four real sadists; their very appearance revealed a type of human akin to the Lombroso criminal type, fully prepared to commit whatever act of violence they thought fit. This applied especially to the Minister of Home Affairs, and to an even greater extent to an obnoxious individual who was in charge of the so-called Ministry of Propaganda, but who in reality quite probably served as the government's evil spirit, and unquestionably bore responsibility for many of the repulsive atrocities that the street mobs, let loose like wild animals, were allowed to commit, unmolested, towards the end of the regime. Inside the government there appears to have been a conflict going on between these two factions, after which the perpetrators of the outrages – the most active of the two – emerged as the victors.

Our own situation in these circumstances, and to an even greater degree that of the Wallenberg operation, seemed more than worrisome. The Wallenberg effort, following a brief respite during the Lakatos regime, was of course geared exclusively towards helping the Jewish element of the population, and was naturally an object of animosity in the eyes of this regime. Our own organisation, which encompassed all those being persecuted and seeking our aid, irrespective of race or religion, would have had an easier time surmounting obstacles if a really clear division had been made between our operations and those of the embassy.

Even considering what was surely an imminent Russian occupation of the capital, such a distinction would have been greatly to our benefit. The Swedish Red Cross enjoyed a long-standing good reputation in Russia, too, and was not hindered by considerations such as those the embassy would suffer from later on, namely its correct relations with the German embassy. I felt quite certain – and could later have this confirmed – that if our country's official representation were to have to suspend its work at a later stage, then a representative of the neutral Swedish Red Cross (with the added advantage of having a good command of the Russian language) could have had excellent prospects of continuing operations undisturbed.

My dear fellow-countrymen would smile somewhat dubiously at what they considered my blue-eyed optimism, claiming that if the embassy folded up, I would live to see that the Red Cross, too, was doomed to give up its work. That my optimism was not altogether unjustified was shown later on when we continued our activities in the new year and for months to come with the consent of the local Russian authorities, in collaboration with the newly-formed Hungarian Red Cross, and with the generous assistance of the new democratic government, until such time as we received the order from Sweden that operations had to cease, handing them over to a recently-established Hungarian–Swedish organisation. At the time that we are now describing, however, I was still attached to the embassy, even though I was for the moment not working there, and in my capacity as Red Cross delegate was directly responsible to its head.

What's more, the new Arrow Cross authorities were naturally eager to lump us all together and treat us all alike: the Swedish aid and assistance was aid to the Jews, whatever you liked to call it! In point of fact there may have been a grain of truth in this contention, because in the dire straits in which the wretched Jews now found themselves under Arrow Cross rule, the urgency of the situation turned their salvation into common ground for both Wallenberg's and our own operations. I was called upon at one point to introduce him to the deputy prime minister, on which occasion he presented what in my view was a fantastical plan to acquire a State credit of 50 million *pengö* to purchase grain, reserving one-quarter for Jewish citizens. This created, I am afraid, a very unfavourable impression and hardly helped in keeping me in the good books of the otherwise indulgent minister, who found the proportions odd and unnecessary, particularly since the Jewish share of the population had never exceeded 6 per cent. For myself I had to concede his point, but at the same time I did not want to disavow my colleague and fellow-countryman.

We had in fact at this time a much more wide-ranging programme, drawn up shortly before the political upheaval, including a plan to set up a hospital primarily intended for refugees not registered in the city and therefore not qualified to receive care from the municipal health authorities. This initiative, however, together with a number of other projects to bring relief to the sick and wounded, met with the greatest difficulties. This was particularly the case when State Secretary von Johann, head of the section at the Ministry of Home Affairs – roughly equivalent to our own Board of Health – was forced to flee to an unknown destination to avoid the fate of so many of his prominent colleagues: imprisonment and deportation to Germany. This man was famous for the exceedingly useful job he had been doing, promising us all imaginable aid in equipment and medical staff. At the same time we had planned and had partly started working on the acquisition of living quarters and soup kitchens for at least a small percentage of the tens of thousands of non-Jewish refugees thronging the roads leading in a northerly and westerly direction towards the capital from areas in the south and east devastated by the hostilities.

This was, in the eyes of the authorities, a point in our favour, but it has to be admitted that the vast majority of orphanages under the aegis of the Red Cross were those of the hated and despised Jewish race. More than anything – and it was plain to see – the clients at our various offices, to almost the same extent as at Wallenberg's, consisted of Jews whose lives were in imminent danger. Those who were not admitted by the Wallenberg organisation because they did not possess family ties or business connections to Sweden would invariably find their way over to us. We were literally overflowing with these applicants, and they formed long, eye-catching queues along the pavement outside our offices. After we had done everything in our power to provide them with letters of protection – as far as they could be of service – or otherwise tried to save them from the clutches of the Germans or the Arrow Cross, the natural consequence of all of this was that our activity also came to be seen as a more or less camouflaged version of an action carried out in support of the Jews.

For my part, at this point in time I had few occasions on which to busy myself with organisational tasks. Above all, I was heavily involved in conducting a series of negotiations instilling confidence in the authorities so that our activities could continue, in spite of the suspicions which were being raised as to our true intentions. The fact that we did finally win through – the 7 July resolution granting us the right to operate was respected – is due in part to the efforts of an old friend, General Consul Barkóczy, who had reluctantly carried on under the new regime until he was eventually sent abroad.

As I had no deputy suitable for the purpose, I was forced to attend to daily requests and petitions, which used up practically all the time left over after the frequent negotiations with the local authorities. Consequently to a certain degree I plainly neglected various areas of the necessary supervision of a large number of our institutions, as well as a measure of collaboration with those members of our embassy with diplomatic status. There was neither time nor opportunity in the long run to maintain contact with our embassy, situated as it was on the other side of the river, and thereby obtain a clearer picture of how they saw our work. My perhaps somewhat naïve optimism led me to believe that we had their full support, even though they could testify with some disquiet to the growing size of our operations. The embassy had shown me their confidence in applying to Stockholm for my appointment as Red Cross delegate. My reports to the Central Committee had been acknowledged and sent off by special courier, whereupon everything appeared to be as it should be.

I had, it must be admitted, felt quite unpleasantly affected when the head of the embassy, referring to Asta Nilsson's continuing separation from our central Red Cross management, declared that she was not in any way to be considered an employee of mine but instead as an equal, independent of me. There followed a short and intensive reminder from my side of the circumstances under which I had requested her assistance in my work from Stockholm, and no more was said on the matter, especially as I had my hands full with other issues more important than purely organisational matters.

I was therefore greatly amazed when one day I was called to see our ambassador to hear that certain criticisms had been levelled at me – from banking institutions and from my own colleagues. In the first of these instances, the matter was put aside after I had been able to reveal that the only banking concern we dealt with was the biggest in the country, the Commercial Bank of Hungary, which had assured us of their benevolent support, and had also actively provided us with generous financial assistance. Later on we were even offered their premises to house our central office – so that the building might enjoy the protection of the Red Cross flag!

My critical colleagues were three in number: principally Ms Nilsson, and then Consul Ekmark and Count Tolstoy. It was an easy matter dealing with Tolstoy: I showed a letter of thanks from him, just received, where he warmly expressed his gratitude for all the assistance I had given him, and particularly for the 25,000 *pengö* placed at his disposal in order to set up the hospital annexe for Russian prisoners-of-war. No reason was given for his so-called 'criticism'. As far as Ekmark was concerned, my rejoinder was that the displeasure was mutual, and we were able to go through the issues at hand in his presence.

I therefore brought up the fact that our agreement had been to maintain daily contact at my offices where he had his own room, still at his disposal. He for his part seemed to have complained that we had been administering the business of acquiring food and had appointed a committee to this end without consulting him. He added that his acute shortage of time prevented him from coming over to our offices, but that he was easy to find for consultations and planning meetings at his own place of work at the Finnish embassy over on the Buda side of the river. Further discussion of this rather trivial question seemed pointless, and the conversation turned to the matter of Asta Nilsson. The head of our embassy now wished to establish the fact that she was *not* to be considered as my departmental head of the orphanages – we were in fact on an equal level, independent of each other, and we were to work separately, each within his/her own field of activity. My natural objection was to the irrational position of having *two* independent Swedish Red Cross organisations in one and the same city, having nothing to do with each other, and that such an arrangement could easily lead to unpleasant consequences – which in due course is exactly what happened. His response was that we were both subordinate to him, and that he was ultimately responsible. I then saw my own position as untenable and respectfully requested my removal as delegate, with the job going to a younger person. Weary after many months of endless work and constant nervous tension, I recommended Ekmark, my friend of many years, as my successor. I had of course counted on him as my deputy (this without success) and for him to succeed me should I meet with any accident. I asked to be able to hand over my mandate and return to the post of embassy 'all-rounder', which I would gladly have done – or else catch a train home, even more gladly!

Our ambassador, however, for once, showed himself to be uncompromising. No question of any dismissal or removal – I was required at my post, and had to steer the ship I myself had launched into port; all that remained for me was to get down off my high horse!

A reorganisation of our activities at this stage could be necessary, and it should be Ekmark's job in his capacity as a practical businessman – he would undoubtedly be able to find a suitable solution to the whole issue. So as not to appear ridiculously obstinate in this matter I agreed to join a committee consisting of Ekmark and Anger from the embassy and Paikert and Vásárhelyi from our organisation. When its proposals were presented for review and approval a couple of days later, all they consisted of was a new version of the division of responsibility and authority that I had firmly rejected. I was then told that we had arrived at an ultimatum and that no other solution was possible from the embassy side, whereupon I renewed my request for a transfer. The answer once again was a firm refusal, accompanied by a heartfelt appeal to my sense of loyalty and duty in finishing the tasks already undertaken. There was no alternative but to go along with the proposal – partly for the sake of a man whose many good qualities had won my admiration, and partly because you can't run off from a job you've taken upon yourself, especially when it now gave signs of becoming even tougher. The fact that one's personal interests were being set aside did not make the decision any more difficult, a decision which in the course of time would prove to be more useful than at that time I neither wished to nor could believe.

For the moment I experienced a certain sense of relief. The tension was gone; I didn't have our 'reorganisation' to think about. A reduction had been decided in the number of premises we had acquired for possible future use but were not utilising at present, in addition to certain changes in our staff situation. I told my staff that until the complete organisation plan was complete and my own powers of authority confirmed, they were to take their instructions from the embassy's representative, Ekmark. For my own part I wished to take advantage of the opportunity to try out my liberated strength on a project, perhaps doomed to failure, but in any case of such importance that it was worth an attempt.

Our close co-operation with both the large Catholic and the two Protestant churches had inspired me with the notion of trying to bring them together to form a united Hungarian Christian front to face up to the violence being perpetrated against the Jewish population. A protest against their violent treatment had been lodged as early as 12 May by the Allied powers with an appeal to Hungary, among others, to withdraw from hostilities and oppose Nazism. It was accompanied by threats of reprisals, but had no effect on the government of that time. Another path chosen, one which gave better results, had been our king's telegram to Horthy on 30 June, who replied saying he 'wished to do everything in his power in the prevailing circumstances to ensure that the principles of humanity and justice be respected'. He had also – we know – to the best of his ability carried out this promise: on 18 July the decision was arrived at to suspend deportations and give Jewish children under a certain age the right to leave the country. Finally, as autumn approached the neutral states' representatives in Budapest had agreed – following some controversy – to issue a rather watered-down appeal to the government when a rumour spread that deportations were to be resumed. That appeal in the current state of affairs was manifestly meaningless.

If now Hungary's Christian churches, however, representing over 90 per cent of the population, would unite in a joint protest couched in the most solemn form and publicly presented to the 'National Leader' personally, it might at least be *possible* that he would reflect upon the fact that he had the entire Christian population against him. After consulting the main representatives of the more important Reform sect as well as those belonging to the lesser Lutheran Church, it was decided to approach the head of the Catholic Church, Cardinal Justinian Serédi. He was to be urged, as *'primus inter pares'*, to pay a personal visit to Szálasi, decked out in full ceremonial robes and backed by the two Protestant bishops, and make it abundantly clear that if the unjust treatment of Jews and Christian Jews was not put an end to, he would have the entire Hungarian Christian community against him. All three churches had to some extent already prepared the ground among their faithful via fairly lame pastoral letters. A particularly upright and courageous Catholic bishop in west Hungary, a true man of principle, Mindszenti, had been bold enough to lead a long procession in the bishopric of Veszprem and testify to his church's firm protest against the brutality that was once more being perpetrated. He had, to the extreme annoyance of his congregation, been remanded in custody, but martyrs are, as is well known, often stronger in deed than those who hold the reins of power. What was essential now was joint public action in the most serious and formal way, hopefully making a far stronger impression on the party concerned than sporadic, intermittent censure and protests had been making up to now. The personal risks involved didn't bother my friends; they were prepared to fight for their beliefs, and they knew too well that throughout history the martyr's crown had often proved to exercise a magical power over people's minds, overcoming that of purely physical violence.

In order to win the Cardinal over, our bishops gave me *carte blanche* to declare them fully prepared to subordinate themselves to his leadership on this question, already a remarkable development in view of the historical and dogma-laden antagonisms which prevailed. Since I was not personally acquainted with the Catholic prelate but did have very good relations with the Papal Nuncio and his secretary, Monsignore Verolino (with whom we had enjoyed quite close collaboration on a social level), I asked them for an introduction and the chance to present the issue. Archbishop Rotta, however, would go no further, he said, than to give his warm blessing to the undertaking, which he heartily supported; for reasons which had to do with the hierarchical system of things he was prevented from attempting to influence the Cardinal's decision. We would, nevertheless, certainly be able to count on immediate admittance to His Eminence, who was known to be at home in his palace in the city of Esztergom, an hour's drive north of Budapest.

This was perfectly true. Accompanying me as a witness was the Protestant dean Wolf-Ordas, later to become a bishop. He had studied on a scholarship at Uppsala, and been fortunate enough to enjoy the friendship of the Swedish Nobel Prize-winning theologian, Nathan Söderblom. The latter's generous and warm personality had made an indelible impression on him, and given him the insight to retain his love for our country and its language, which he still had a good command of both in speech and writing. Although it turned out that our arrival almost coincided with their dinner time, we were immediately met by His Eminence who gave us an hour of his time in conversation, expressing his admiration for the Swedish Red Cross work in Hungary, of which he appeared to be well-informed. When it came to the key issue, however, he initially showed a tough and unsentimental line. For one thing he had already dispatched a written protest to Szálasi which had had no effect and which therefore gave him to understand that further action was pointless. For another, he plainly considered a public action together with the Protestant churches a grave and dubious issue without precedent, from a general Catholic viewpoint both in theory and in practice.

However, confronted by the arguments we put forward, he gradually softened up: it concerned breaking the ice and creating a common church front establishing a strong authoritative line in dealing with the current powers-that-were and – it was to be hoped – in eventual negotiations with a subsequent regime of a totally different type. The leading figures in the Protestant churches had declared themselves willing to submit to the primacy of the much more powerful Catholic Church as being superior both in rank and influence. Everything would be carefully prepared, and for His Eminence the result would be a deed unique in the country's history – a joint action on the part of the churches, in conflict with each other for centuries, something which would ensure that his name would go down in history.

These were big words coming from a simple citizen, strictly speaking an irrelevant individual, but they appeared to produce an effect, and were energetically seconded by the sturdy presence of my Protestant companion. He didn't waste the opportunity to show his wide knowledge of current affairs by making reference to the situation in Norway where the Catholic Church, a tiny minority, had not hesitated in jeopardising its very existence by whole-heartedly joining the large Protestant majority's relentless campaign against Nazi crimes, in spite of the serious risks involved.

We finally arrived at a point where the Cardinal no longer seemed reluctant to agree to a joint action, one which would not only take the form of a fresh protest in writing but also a personal and public appeal arguing the case in no uncertain terms. Unquestionably it would also be picked up by the Allied and world press and thus work in favour of the country's interests at any future peace conference: the victorious powers would know that a collective Christian community in Hungary via its representatives had put up a stubborn fight for its humanitarian and freedom ideals, irrespective of the hazards which might threaten their private lives.

When these arguments had been presented and developed, an almost pleading look came over the Cardinal's face and he said: 'But I can have a few days' reflection, can't I?'

'Of course! Especially if your Eminence replies by saying as the lady did when being courted "it won't be no, whatever the case"!'

When we got back to the car, the Protestant vicar and I thought the game was half over with a win for us, and we congratulated each other on what we hoped we had achieved. The truth was, however, that we were soon going to see that it was we who had finished up on the losing side.

After waiting five days we returned by car and were given the news by the primate's chief of staff that His Eminence was unavailable to attend through 'temporary ill-health', but that he had personally composed a new letter of protest which had been sent the day before through a reliable channel to Szálasi and should therefore be in his hands by now. I was given a copy together with a personal letter couched in the nicest language where the Cardinal suggested that the Protestant leaders – there was no question of being 'brothers in Christ' – might announce their support should they so feel inclined. To begin with, however, this was not of course technically possible since the original copy had already been sent off (probably in order to present us with a *fait accompli*), and then again it was hardly feasible on account of the very wording: a long-winded treatise of six closely-written pages without any bite to it whatever. Our own bishops had to confine themselves to a short, clear but firm protest – also unfortunately merely in writing – on behalf of their own churches. The joint action envisaged remained but an empty gesture.

Szálasi, who to be sure was no voluptuous tyrant or sadistic criminal but merely a poor soul obsessed by delusions of grandeur (like his counterpart in Oslo), found himself more and more thrust into the arms of his desperate henchmen. He issued a decree containing a number of new, exceedingly severe clauses referring to Jews, and totally gave in to the Germans' demands for delivery of human flesh in a manner which made the memory of the brutal deportations early in the summer pale into insignificance.

In the cold, damp November weather with rain and wind lashing town and countryside alike, the wretched Jews, young and old, men and women, were driven through Budapest's streets to an assembly point on the outskirts of the city. There, exposed to the elements and without food except what they were able to take with them in their pockets, they were obliged to wait until such time as they were arranged into endless lines and prodded along the country road by Hungarian soldiers towards the border with Germany.

On a third journey towards Esztergom, which I shall never be able to erase from my memory, I saw half of the roadway filled for mile after mile with these poor creatures, plodding along in the dirt and filth, weighed down by their puny bundles, in which they carried the few possessions left to them. Spotting our car and its conspicuous Swedish flag and Red Cross symbol, many among them raised a heart-rending cry for help and rescue, but were immediately silenced by the soldiers, who brutally forced the bolder among them back into line with their rifle butts.

Followed by the sullen gaze of pitch-black eyes, half-crazed by their desperate condition, we proceeded along this muddy highway along which these wretched beings were made to wander, day after day, for hundreds of kilometres, on the way to an unknown destination. Our task on this trip was to find the brother of one of our employees who had been dragged away, and quite remarkably we managed to find him. Nonetheless, every attempt to free him on the basis of a letter of protection which we had issued ended in failure. The divisional commander politely but firmly refused to hand him over without an order from a higher authority. To obtain such an order and get back in time before he had disappeared over the border seemed almost impossible, and the brother beside me wept inconsolably like a child. Not even a man's tears can move a pillar of stone.

The same appalling spectacle was repeated day after day, week after week, until the end of the year when out of the dark clouds of the ashes of warfare flashes of lightning rained down on our unhappy city and finally put our tormentors to flight. During these two months all our lives were in mortal danger, both at the embassy and the Red Cross. Raoul Wallenberg was as a knight in shining armour, without fear and without reproach, performing superhuman acts to come to the aid of the Jews, hunted down like animals as they were, while our own staff, in charge of civil protection matters under the brave leadership of my wife, were not daunted either by the constant threat of capture and death. On both our fronts we felt an inner joy that our passports and letters of protection, although they didn't always bring unconditional liberty to the holder, were still in the majority of cases respected, at least for the time being, rescuing thousands from the most dreadful of fates.

Both during and after the failed attempt to unite the three Christian churches for an effective intervention, my own chief task personally was that of saving human lives – everything else had to take a back seat. This partly took the shape of typing out and signing masses of letters of protection – at this juncture without paying too much attention to the respective qualifications of each individual – and partly of hiding people who because of their position were in particular danger of being arrested, using the homes of trustworthy friends whose houses and flats were protected with Red Cross identification plaques. A couple of Jewish families stayed at my small apartment for weeks on end, preferring during the heavy bombing to risk their lives high up in the building rather than run the risk of discovery down in the basement shelter. There was also a Hungarian colonel sent by the embassy (together with a number of other people), to save him from certain execution for his co-operation with the Allies. Another such refugee was the proprietor of the city's biggest department store as well as several hotels and institutions on Margaret Island which he had generously placed at the disposal of the Red Cross.

A number of our vehicles were constantly on the move rescuing people in this way, night after night, moving from place to place, as long as we were able to keep them under our control. Among the drivers were a couple of courageous lieutenants who risked life and limb by refusing to join the army in its move to the west. Similarly, a number of high-ranking civil servants had been ordered to join the ministry's move from Budapest to smaller cities near the border with Germany and out of the war zone; they preferred to remain in hiding at various places at night, and work for the Red Cross during the day in our premises, which, we believed, were safe from attack.

As civil order gradually collapsed and more and more street hooligans found their way into the official registers of the Arrow Cross party, the protection and shelter we believed we could offer became more and more of a delusion. One fine November day, when I'd spent a couple of hours in the morning strolling up to the heights on the Buda side of the river, with its spectacular view over a city still relatively unravaged by warfare and a countryside reminiscent of the Arno valley around Florence, I returned to find my office brimming over with people desperately seeking help, a long queue stretching out into the street. In their midst an Arrow Cross detachment led by the party's 'district boss' wanted to arrest and carry off all the able-bodied Jews. I physically dragged this 'boss' to the telephone and had him receive orders from the ministry to vacate our premises immediately – we were still at that time blessed, in our capacity as an officially-acknowledged relief organisation, with the protection of the highest authorities.

After driving the mischief-makers out and managing to get the sceptical policemen who had been posted there on my side, I wished to have their assistance in dispersing the entire rabble. A high-ranking police officer, who deep inside was really sympathetic to our cause and who later would be of great service to us, declared that he was within his rights in affording the building and the driveway protection from trespassers, but that out on the streets power was in the hands of the Arrow Cross in their guise as militiamen – an extremely odd state of affairs, we thought, since any old troublemaker could apply for membership in the party, be given an armband and a rifle, and take his place as a 'guardian of law and order'.

A scuffle broke out between me and the stubborn leader who wouldn't leave with his bunch of toughs but persevered in his attempt to get at his would-be victims, but it all ended without any bloodshed. Without my knowing, however, a call had been put through to the embassy to the effect that I was in mortal danger. Very considerately, the head of our embassy swiftly made his way over to our offices with two colleagues to rescue me, but by that time I was already seated at my desk filling out letters of protection with photographs and relevant details supplied by my staff for the applicants who were eagerly waiting to be served in order to escape being dragged off by the mob. The ambassador expressed his discontent, which I could well understand, with this 'production line'. I then, however, introduced as one of our staff a retired high-ranking police officer, whose recommendation produced such an effect that the ambassador took a seat at the desk and in no time was signing an assortment of urgent material himself!

The overcrowding that took place, however, prevented a number of people with genuine claims for our protection from being attended to, and they were forced to leave empty-handed. Others whose consciences were not so crystal-clear took advantage of the chaos and got hold of a bunch of forms which they filled in with false signatures, and then either made use of themselves or gave to others in exchange for cash. The damage done to our disinterested charitable organisation was not evident until later on when the falsehoods were discovered, and quite naturally this had a negative effect on how reliable the authentic documents really were. Similar situations arose to a greater and more damaging extent with the Wallenberg 'protective passports', which were held in higher esteem than ours and were therefore 'quoted' at a higher 'rate of exchange'. On the other hand, my incredibly energetic colleague with his diplomatic influence and financial backing accomplished so much more for the general good than we were able to.

He despatched vehicles, or went with them, along the roads leading to the border with Germany, to gather up whole columns of *protégés* who had been detained despite the fact that they were in possession of authentic official Swedish identification documents. In addition – and this is perhaps even more important – he managed to secure the assignment of a large number (thirty-two in all) of six-storey buildings in a certain area of the city (we succeeded in acquiring eight) where the *protégés* of both our organisations could be accommodated. In this way they avoided being confined to the vast ghetto where all the other Jews in the city were held before joining the ever-increasing multitudes awaiting deportation. In command at the Wallenberg premises were the exceedingly active Sixten von Bayer and his splendid Dutch wife; our own buildings were run with the greatest care and attention by my own wife and her assistants, who were able to exchange any dangerous fraudulent documents that were found for new, authentic ones. The Swedish buildings thereby acquired a reputation for impeccable care, which was not, however, the case where others belonging to the 'international ghetto' were concerned, and inside which Swiss, Spanish, Portuguese and Papal *protégés* were housed. As opposed to conditions within the Hungarian ghetto, all of these enjoyed the 'privilege' of being able to walk out into the street freely and make their necessary purchases of food at least for some hours during the day. Naturally we lent what assistance we could in this respect with what we could spare. Total safety out in the street was not of course to be expected; incidents occurred where the ghetto inhabitants were seized by Arrow Cross on the lookout for victims, had their letters of protection torn up, were robbed of whatever money they had on them, and were dragged off to an internment camp from which it would be nigh on impossible to retrieve them. A German officer in command there assured me that if we could station some people there who could guarantee that the victim in question really had been in possession of genuine Swedish documents before being robbed of them, they would immediately be freed. We did not, however, have at our disposal sufficiently 'Aryan' colleagues – no question of others being considered – who would be willing and brave enough to undertake such a far from risk-free task.

At the same time as these incidents – and probably in part as a result of their being generally successful – a number of prearranged assaults by Arrow Cross mobs began to take place at places where our *protégés* had been living for weeks relatively undisturbed. A couple of these assaults will serve to give an idea of the prevailing situation at this point in time.

Late one evening – it was past midnight – my wife and her colleagues were at their desks in one of our convents typing out 'documents of protection' for 200 nuns. A belated transport of food from the provinces arrived, and as the gates were being opened a score of heavily-armed Arrow Cross seized the opportunity to force their way in with the intention of seizing any Jews concealed within. A few of them were manifestly under the influence of drink while they all behaved in a frightening manner, slamming their dog-whips down on the table, shouting and swearing and creating havoc.

'What's this, then!' they yelled on catching sight of the photographs and documents lying on the tables. 'So this is a nice little factory for these confounded Jewish documents.' Everybody was to prove his or her identity, and the entire building was to be searched. 'We know you've got a bunch of Jews hidden away here!'

This was indeed the case, and now they had to be saved from being hauled off into slavery or annihilation. The courageous nuns wanted to intervene and showed the letter of protection referring to the convent, issued by both the Red Cross and the embassy. 'Aren't you ashamed of having anything to do with Jews?' bellowed the leader, demanding to go through the building straightaway.

Why, by all means, the ladies agreed, here were no adult Jews, only children, who were exempted from deportation in accordance with current regulations. Then began a tour of the extensive premises – the orphanage was shown and all the doors unlocked and opened, and not a Jew was to be seen. Reaching the danger area it was explained that here *clausura* prevailed, a Latin expression the implication of which every Catholic clearly understood: a space sacred to the inhabitants of the convent and absolutely without access to any outsider. This *pia fraus* – 'pious fraud' – was a complete success. The interlopers left empty-handed! While these good ladies were performing their rescue operation, however, some of the other rogues got into the office which were unoccupied for the moment, grabbed as many completed letters of protection as they could find, together with the cash till and the few small articles of Hungarian jewellery my wife possessed and had kept in her handbag. Everything was stuffed into a little rucksack they had brought with them, and in the relief everybody felt as they prepared to leave it didn't occur to our people to ask what they were carrying – they wouldn't have got an honest reply in any case! On reporting the theft the following day at the Party district headquarters they had the remarkable luck to be attended to by a commander who was a devout Catholic and whose sister at one point in time had been educated in that very convent. He registered the complaint and promised everything would be done to put things right. Among the Party's principles, he said, was an order strictly forbidding any kind of assault on Church property – if only the rascals could be identified, they would be severely punished . . . They had of course – unfortunately – failed to leave their addresses! Nevertheless, he called on them a few days later bringing a small sum of money (probably stolen somewhere else) plus a quantity of letters of protection in a torn and filthy condition; the jewellery, though, had not been retrieved.

On another occasion I was myself involved in a nasty tussle at the same place. They had phoned me for help, and on arrival I found the entrance blocked by a bevy of Arrow Cross men. By that time we had managed to arrange for a policeman to be on guard inside the building day and night. The constable on duty opened the door to me but refused to allow the besiegers in, whereupon they threatened to use the hand grenades they wore in belts around their bodies.

'Not until you show me a warrant from the Ministry of Home Affairs will I let you in!' the policeman resolutely exclaimed.

'We've got one!' was the response, and they waved a sheet of paper in front of us. When it was shown to us through a slot in

103

the doorway, however, it turned out to be no more than a written order signed by the head of their local district.

The policeman sneered at them, threatening to shoot anyone who tried to blow up the entrance. The mob retired to the other side of the street, went into a huddle, and finally sent a messenger off to the Ministry.

The brave nuns made use of the rather long time that elapsed by hiding their adult Jews in the drains and other nooks and crannies in the building. Gaining time is gaining a good deal, we thought, and we did indeed gain it.

When the messenger returned an hour or two later he had a genuine ministerial order authorising an inspection of the convent, and I ordered the door to be opened for the Arrow Cross to enter. Together with the venerable abbess and her proud and brave deputy I stood at the centre of the staircase, where we met the chief of the posse with a sharp protest at their disturbing the peace of the convent and abusing the dignity and significance of the Swedish Red Cross identification markings. It had no effect, of course, and a search was begun of the premises. Their haul was confined, however, to three poor old women and half a dozen adolescent girls, who were taken away to the ghetto. It was naturally painful enough not to be able to do anything, but things could have been so much worse if they had got their hands on all the others who were concealed.

This incident and other similar episodes were merely the small beginning to a series of violent assaults of a different type which subsequently took place. The Arrow Cross headquarters were situated at a major road junction opposite the Social Sisters' central building, where we had succeeded in obtaining a safe haven for a hundred or so persecuted people. They included the celebrated dramatist Eugen Heltai and his wife; the senior physician Professor Rusznyák, who enjoyed a high reputation throughout Hungary, and who had suffered a lot during his deportation to Germany, but who had escaped, however, and now served as our own senior physician; a few prominent businessmen plus one of Wallenberg's colleagues,

closely related to a partner of his back in Sweden. The head of
the institution, Margit Schlachta, was one of our most reliable
and skilled helpers, and was widely known throughout
Hungary as one of the country's leading figures concerning
social issues. One day I suddenly got a call from her: 'They're
here now . . . please come and help us!'

On my arrival I found the building surrounded by armed
Arrow Cross men, but managed to gain entry on producing my
identification papers. I was warned, however, that I was
welcome to go in, but if I tried to leave they would shoot me
down! There was uproar inside. Weeping men, women and
children sat packed like sardines watched over by Arrow Cross
people brandishing pistols, rifles and hand grenades. Margit
Schlachta alone remained calm and collected. She had also
phoned Monsignor Verolino at the papal nunciate, and he was
soon with us. Together we managed to persuade a guard to
bring the militia district chief, a dreadful individual with a
jutting chin, glassy eyes and the world's sweatiest hands. He
dare not refuse to let me go out and phone – the telephone in
the building was now out of order. I got hold of Wallenberg,
who soon arrived equipped with an order from the Ministry of
Home Affairs forbidding the detention of anyone in possession
of Swedish documents and obliging the guard to leave and
await further orders. We saw to it that they all left with their
ugly leader at their head. Sister Margit offered consolation to
those whose nerves were on end over further persecution, and
when it got dark she helped a number of them escape and look
for other, less conspicuous places to hide; not for a moment
did she lose her elevated state of spiritual calm.

Later that evening the air-raid sirens sounded as usual. The
persecuted flock, which had now been rescued, gathered in the
basement shelter and a service of thanksgiving was held, led
by Margit Schlachta. When afterwards I gave her a hug and
planted a kiss on her forehead, a lady sitting close by
exclaimed:

'What's it like, kissing an angel? If you've never done it
before, you've done it now!'

'Indeed, indeed, a true angel!' was the cry from all around, and in that semi-dark locality lit by a flickering paraffin lamp a forest of thin white hands stretched up in the air in acclamation. For my part, I had hardly ever experienced such a gripping religious moment before. You might have been in one of Rome's early Christian catacombs during the terrible years of persecution.

Not even Sister Margit's heroic soul was capable of struggling through to achieve final peace and quiet for these poor tormented creatures. A fresh nocturnal raid followed some time later, and any pretence at discipline was abandoned. The remaining elderly people were forcefully removed and the premises plundered, despite a hazardous attempt to intervene on our part. Similarly our attempts to protect the Hermine convent nearby were also in vain and the inhabitants were hauled away and the place ransacked – all I managed to achieve was that they left the nuns in peace. There were also reported raids carried out on our wonderful Sacré Coeur convent, as a result of which my wife together with her best assistant, at great risk to their lives brought all the Jewish children by long and difficult routes through the city to one of our Swedish premises, where they at last could escape the risk of ending up in the prison-like ghetto. My wife even managed to arrange a Swedish yuletide party when the repression was at its worst, and a speech was given in Swedish by one of my former university students – a woman who a mere three weeks later fell victim to a shell fired from the Buda side after she returned to her apartment not far from our own following the Russians' capture of Pest.

It was in one of our monasteries – the French Frères de Marie – that I very nearly came to a bad end. We'd had both an orphanage and a hiding place for adults there: one of these was the son of the former prime minister Kállay. A written report had been sent us by an anonymous person alleging that the Gestapo had emptied the building of its inhabitants and arrested all the monks. I hurried there and was let in by a German soldier, who locked the door behind me and asked me my business.

'I'm looking for Frère Albert,' was my brief reply.

'He's not here. But come with me. Are you French?'

'No, why? I'm Swedish.'

'Follow me anyway.'

He grabbed my arm and tried to shove me into a room where a lot of people were gathered, evidently men and women who had come with a similar purpose and who had been admitted but not allowed to leave as they were supposedly to be the monks' 'partners in crime'.

'You've no right at all to detain me!' I protested, and thrust my documents in front of him.

'We are merely following orders. Come with me now!'

'I will not be forced – take me to your commander.'

'He's not here at the moment.'

'Then phone him. You'll pay for it if anything happens to me.'

'Do you know anyone among our leaders?'

I named three or four *Sturmbannführer* I'd heard about, and one at least should know my name. A call was made, and as luck would have it this was the one who answered. The situation was desperate enough: if I fell into the hands of the Gestapo, goodness knows how long I'd be sitting there. The German spelled his way laboriously through one of my papers and read it over the telephone. On hearing the reply he stood to attention and uttered into the receiver: 'Yes sir, right, *Herr Sturmbannführer!*'

And to me he said: 'You are at liberty and we beg your pardon for the mistake.'

'You have done your duty,' I said, 'but you can see now that it was I who was right!'

The soldier led me politely out through the door, but when I stepped into my car where my wife was anxiously waiting, I received a fair old telling-off: 'You're never to do this sort of thing again,' she scolded me. 'We have to deal with people we *can* possibly save, no others . . .'

She was probably right. Women always are . . . Though, in this particular case, I think not. The monks came through unscathed, without our intervention. A few months later we heard that our friends had had to suffer hunger and violent assault in heavy doses, but that they all nevertheless survived.

While these incidents were being played out as rather unimportant yet significant omens of pogroms to come, we waited in vain for the reorganisation which had been announced by the embassy. Week after week had passed, and our reminders appeared to be having no effect. It must be admitted, however, that the men and women working there really had their work cut out for them and there was hardly time over for anything else. Once an alarm was raised that the Arrow Cross had broken into the stores we shared with the chocolate manufacturers Stühmers, and were in the process of ransacking them. Two of our officials hurried there but were unable to stop them, and the usual flow of protests began. And so it went on.

Wallenberg worked day and night. Ms Nilsson looked after her own business, undoubtedly to the best of her ability, but we never received any report of her work, except when one or other of her orphanages begged us for foods, which we duly supplied as far as our provisions allowed. The first soup kitchen was performing splendidly, and a couple of hundred Hungarian refugees were being fed daily practically cost-free. There was still no word from home of financial assistance, for if we had got any we would immediately have started more soup kitchens.

We wanted now – unpretentiously – to establish our own hospital to add to those we were already contributing to. It was launched with a score of beds and full medical equipment, and was installed in a large building at *Ullöi ut*, which was the hospital district of the city. The building, which went under the name of *Heinrich udvar*, belonged to the country's largest hardware business, with space for living accommodation and storage. After moving there we remained for good, and in the course of time, through the remarkable vicissitudes of life, we would see the premises develop into the Swedish Red Cross' impregnable fortress and foothold, at a later date the headquarters of our successor, the Swedish–Hungarian Society, as well as the social section of the apostolic nuncio, which co-operated with us. I shall have more to say about this later on.

It was there that our chief physician, Professor Rusznyák, referred to earlier, moved in together with his family. After fleeing the Social Sisters' premises, which had been evacuated, he had crept from one hiding place to another and finally found shelter here. He assumed responsibility for health care at our own hospital and inspection duties at another dozen or so in the city with which we collaborated, after they had passed under our protection and at times received certain amounts of food and medicine from us.

In order to increase both the technical and financial resources for our relief work, a measure of co-operation was begun with the Portuguese embassy, whose ambassador had withdrawn and quite simply gone home, leaving a Hungarian consul-general in charge. An agreement was reached with this man to the effect that we would endeavour to make use of a small but charming mansion on the Buda side of the river, the property of Count Paul Esterházy, the country's largest landowner and a former Swedish language student of mine and still a very good friend. I had previously made a similar suggestion to our own embassy in the hope that we thereby could save its exceptionally fine collection of *objets d'art* from looting and destruction, but my suggestion was turned down. Now I might be able to use property on behalf of a Portuguese Red Cross unit, capable of providing both the financial means and a workforce. A plan was drawn up of how to apply for a Hungarian government licence to establish a new Red Cross organisation in Budapest. It was decided that the best way to go about it would be to use what in that era was known as the 'petticoat method'. My wife agreed to try and win the confidence of the Foreign Minister's pleasant but somewhat conceited young spouse, the Baroness Kemény. She was quite successful, and the way was now open to the Baron's own office in a foreign ministry now almost completely empty.

The minister turned out to be a very young and quite pleasant man, naturally adorned with the characteristic Arrow Cross green scarf, but in all other respects and unlike his Party companions a perfectly civil person, in both senses of the word. He found it feasible that our request might be granted, and appeared to consider the Portuguese Red Cross to be an organisation already in existence, but for an official acknowledgement he required a joint statement on the part of Sweden and Portugal recognising the new Hungarian regime.

'We have good reason to expect the establishment of diplomatic relations with the neutral countries,' he said, 'after the hopes our enemies entertained of seeing us knocked out have gone up in smoke. We've already been in power for a longer period than our predecessor was able to enjoy,' he added with a slight but overweening smile.

The truth was that Hungary already had a diplomatic representative in Stockholm: two, in fact. One was Ullein-Reviczky, who had disassociated himself from the Sztójay regime which seized power after the March *coup*, and the other one was Parcher, who seemed to have done the same thing following the October *putsch*. Neither was therefore of use to the Arrow Cross, who were not supported by any of the Hungarian diplomats in any of the neutral countries. As a result the regime in Budapest had declared these gentlemen – of whom there were twenty – traitors to their homeland, and in their absence sentenced them to death by hanging. This hardly constituted a suitable platform for resuming diplomatic relations.

Sensibly enough, our Arrow Cross baron refrained from following up this line of thought after I'd explained that I did not have the authority to do anything in this direction, and after I had pointed out that we were here faced with a social issue concerning relief for people in distress, problems we could perhaps solve regardless of political differences. He instead made two more reasonable requests, which were really more like commands! One was to deliver a list of all our staff and the premises we were using, whereupon I took care to suggest that such a list would for the present be fairly useless as well as misleading since our embassy had still not completed the reorganisation it had planned, with all the changes that that implied . . . My real reason, of course, was that I wanted to avoid handing over names and addresses which could lead the Arrow Cross gangs straight to their scenes of murder and robbery. His other request was for *every* foreign relief organisation – he mentioned a French and a Spanish one too – to be brought into close co-operation with the leading lights at the Hungarian Red Cross. There were no objections to this proposal, in theory, while in practice it was manifestly unfeasible for reasons we shall presently see.

Very soon afterwards representatives of all the relief organisations working in Budapest were summoned to the Foreign Ministry by Barkóczy's closest colleague and successor, Consul-General Medgyesi, who happened to be a friend of ours who shared our views, but who had avoided slinking off at the time of the coup, getting caught, and then being treated as a traitor to the holy cause. There, in one of the ministry's abandoned rooms and offices, we were gathered – representatives of the Papal Nuncio, the International and the Swedish Red Cross, and those of Portugal, France and Spain. At the front was the Hungarian Red Cross which presided over the meeting under the leadership of an Arrow Cross bigwig with the authority of a commissar. A snotty-nosed young doctor, he sat like a recent *parvenu* on the scene in this multi-lingual gathering, alone representing the regime's point of view, capable of expressing himself only in Hungarian, with a smattering of French and German thrown in. He read out a verbose decree from the National Leader setting out the conditions for our *raison d'être*: a committee was to be formed to share out work among us under the direction of the commissar himself.

Two difficulties surfaced at once. One related to a statement made by the delegate of the *Comité International de la Croix Rouge*, a rather bizarre Swiss businessman in Budapest called Fr. Born. Early in the summer he had told me he intended rescuing 300,000(!) Jews from deportation, and proposed I arrange with our Central Committee in Stockholm for a couple of million dollars to be placed at his royal disposal.

His opposition to the decree concerned the fact that by its statutes the International Red Cross was prevented from collaborating with individual national Red Cross units, much less subject itself to the authority of one of them, in this case the Hungarians. Total silence enveloped the room, broken only when I quietly pointed out that the very honourable National Leader appeared to have issued a decree it was evidently impossible to obey. The commissar's embarrassing position, which was due to his manifest ignorance as to what the International Committee really was, took a further turn for the worse when he was compelled to explain that the entire managerial body of the Hungarian Red Cross, its institutions and its equipment, were being moved out of the capital to the west. At this stage it was finally decided the desired committee would indeed be formed but under the leadership of the International Red Cross delegate as the natural choice for such a role. A new meeting would be held a few days later at its very elegant headquarters, a handsome villa on the Buda side, which had once been offered us but which we fortunately refrained from taking over – a week or two later it was blown to smithereens by a bomb!

At this meeting, which would be the last but one, our commissar friend informed us that he had been instructed to leave the city within three days and establish his operations near the border with Germany; the hospitals were to be evacuated and could be placed at the disposal of the various Red Cross organisations, but emptied of beds, food and medical equipment! The representative of the Papal Nuncio, a Catholic priest of that rare type of finely cultivated person you sometimes happen on in southern countries, announced that he had over a million *pengö* he could use for the purchase and storage of urgently needed medical supplies, but that he had been denied permission to buy them. The Portuguese, who had still not obtained written confirmation acknowledging their organisation, asked how they could go about their work and its financial support when the Hungarian Red Cross requisitioned all available equipment for the benefit of the retreating army columns. I made so bold as to remark that if the civil population, three-fourths of which were non-Jewish, was abandoned and left to certain death from starvation and disease, they would be forced in the end to turn to the advancing foe for relief. The retort from the Arrow Cross was nothing more than a cynical declaration that every inhabitant of our capital city who didn't leave escorted by the army should be prepared to take the consequences. How they were to be evacuated when all transport had either been commandeered by the Germans or requisitioned by the Arrow Cross, nobody knew; most of our own vehicles had already disappeared that way. To put it mildly, the entire proceedings were nothing short of a macabre farce, and we never saw another trace of the commissar. Of his two deputies, posted in Buda and Pest respectively, the former retired to private life, and the latter, a dry old armchair general, was only seen once more at our last meeting, when everything was on the verge of collapse. Our so-called committee also disintegrated in the storm.

Finally, sentence was passed on our own Red Cross organisation: the Arrow Cross regime forbade further activity. The upshot of it all was as follows: in a *note verbale* to our embassy, Baron Kemény had repeated his demand for full particulars concerning our staff and our premises. As this might involve dangerous risks for all of us, after consultations with our head of embassy I wrote to the Baron repeating the same reasons as I had offered before, adding that as soon as the new organisation of our activities was definite we would accede to his requests. The purpose behind this was quite simply to gain a short respite for our operations in those places which hitherto had escaped the series of raids and assaults. The so-called reorganisation was still an open question, but the embassy's note in reply tallied with this notion. The subterfuge was a bit too obvious, however, as often happens in diplomacy, and we got the worst of it. Following a fresh demand in the shape of a circular sent to all concerned, we received a call from the Foreign Ministry stating that if the details requested were not handed in by 4pm the same day, the Swedish Red Cross's licence would be immediately withdrawn and if its operations continued they would be regarded as illegal.

It came of no help that on the stroke of four I delivered an account of the purpose of our work, its division into the various branches, what had hitherto been achieved and what was in the pipeline, together with a request for a deferment in providing lists of members of staff and premises. It appears that that very same evening the Ministerial Council decided on a ban on further activity by the Swedish Red Cross.

We were now outlawed and thereby dangerously exposed to any kind of arbitrary assault. Two or three of our more prominent premises, the Central Office itself and the sec-retariat as well as our special protection section were immediately invaded and looted. Every attempt to break into our ultra-modern safe failed, and it was far too heavy to cart away. The keys to it were of course demanded, but fortunately I had deposited them with our embassy and they were never handed over. The safe was proof against hand grenades, and therefore its contents of money and valuables could be secure until such time, far into the New Year, as we were able to see to them in peace and quiet. The plundered premises were guarded and put under lock and key, and a sentry saw to it that nobody entered. One evening late at night during this period, however, we did receive a message from the head of the local police district – a man loyal to us and also in possession of one of our letters of protection – who on his own initiative allowed us to enter the building so we could see for ourselves that the safe remained undisturbed. Without the keys, however, and unable to sneak away with such a heavy object, we were forced to leave it where it was and trust to our luck, which as it turned out did not desert us.

The same cannot be said, regrettably, of the various stores of food deposited at different places around the city by the embassy and by ourselves, which were systematically plundered. Our Jewish staff were in grave danger, as were those who inhabited the so-called 'protected' living accommodation as soon as they poked their noses outside the door. Even indoors, there was nothing now to stop the Arrow Cross, who showed not the slightest respect for the Red Cross symbol and identification plaques. A similar situation afflicted Wallenberg's numerous staff, a very small number of whom could be transferred to his Pest central office. Practically all of them were Jewish, but they did enjoy the benefit of belonging to the 'Royal Swedish Embassy's Humanitarian Department', which should have afforded them a greater measure of security than what they could expect from the Red Cross, now declared illegal. Yet even this protection was becoming more and more illusory after the Arrow Cross's appetite had been whetted following their unpunished raids on the stores.

As far as other 'unprotected' Jewish lives were concerned, they were, indeed, utterly unprotected. Shooting was heard in the streets all over the place, especially after dark. While earlier attempts were mostly made to seek out able-bodied Jews and drag them off for slave labour, it was now considered more suitable to drive them in the direction of the Danube quayside, mow them down in an orgy of shooting, and throw the corpses into the river. Some who had survived the shooting swam badly injured to the embankment, and were shot again, or were fortunate enough to escape under cover of darkness. Raids took place at night throughout the city, and when among the tens of thousands of letters of protection – particularly the enormous number of Swiss ones – clearly fraudulent papers were found, this naturally led to a sort of inflation process whereby the authentic documents lost a deal of their value, more or less in the same way in which genuine banknotes come under suspicion when counterfeits appear.

All power to the gunmen! When the roughest customers could get hold of weapons and badges simply by applying for party membership, it was no wonder that murder and plunder raged throughout the city. Later it was made plain what sort of people had been roaming the streets under the guise of militiamen. Following the Russian occupation a number of those among the dead and the captured were found with both Arrow Cross and Soviet emblems, intended to be shown for identification according to which way the wind was blowing. Every eventuality had been taken into consideration, but fate overtook treachery in the end.

At this time we were largely out of touch with the embassy on the Buda side of the river, where Asta Nilsson also had her main quarters. One of the seven bridges spanning the Danube had already been blown up in November – 'by mistake', it was claimed – plunging a number of crowded trams as well as numerous pedestrians into the river. Another – the northern railway bridge – had been hit earlier on by a bomb, and I myself saw one of the spans collapsing into the water through my binoculars. A similar fate might well be suffered by any of the other bridges, all of which had been wired with explosives and presented a welcome target for the frequent, daily air raids. These air raids did us a minor favour, nonetheless, by forcing the Arrow Cross ruffians down into the shelters for a few hours at least. Dangerous as they were, the air raids seemed to bother us less than other matters. With death lurking at every corner, there was little room for choice.

On a chance meeting with our consul Ekmark, who undoubtedly had been doing his level best on behalf of both the embassy and the Swedish community, most of whom lived on the Buda side, and who for this reason had had little time to devote to Red Cross matters, he made my wife and me the kindly offer of a couple of rooms in a fortress-like building which he wanted to furnish for the benefit of the Swedish contingent. I declined the offer with many thanks, for I saw myself still as the captain of a small ship battling against the elements, my duty being to remain at my post until the entire 'crew' had either perished or been saved. Most of our operations were confined to Pest, east of the river, where most of the atrocities were being perpetrated. Nor did Wallenberg appear to have considered entrenching himself in Buda, which it transpired later would have been little better than suicide.

The entire Swedish community was invited by the ambassador to a 'simple lunch' at the embassy on Christmas Day. When I phoned on the 23rd accepting and thanking him for the invitation, and inquiring after the well-being of our people on that side of the river, I was assured that in the circumstances all was well, and we were heartily welcome to the festive occasion.

That night, however, pandemonium broke loose. At four in the morning of Christmas Eve a gang of Arrow Cross mobsters penetrated the embassy building, committing a series of violent acts. Clothes, food and valuables were snatched, and the staff were put under guard. The marauding horde then made for the neighbouring Finnish embassy where our department charged with looking after the affairs of other combatant nations was based. They carried off as much as they could lay their hands on of personal property, vehicles and petrol, from here and from other premises close by. Of the embassy's diplomatic corps it would appear that only the two youngest members, Berg and Carlsson, were there, and they managed to escape before the Arrow Cross gang returned. The two ladies who were there – Ms Bauer and another Ms Nilsson – were removed to the Jewish ghetto, however, and it wasn't until the evening that the International Red Cross was able to intervene and have them set free. It was later, too, that we obtained a rather confusing description of what had happened, and I am therefore unable to be more precise. Not until New Year's Eve did we succeed in regaining the telephone connection (it would be the last) with the embassy, and we were obliged to limit our conversation to plain and simple greetings of well-being and happiness since without question all the calls were being tapped. In the meantime the embassy was certainly subjected to further abuse, about which I have no further knowledge as every link with them was cut off for the following two months.

For our part, we continued our operations as best we could, defying the Arrow Cross ban, between bombing raids and shellfire. We brought food to the people in the buildings signposted as Swedish-protected, and in institutions we were co-operating with. We gave freely of our aid and our sympathy as best we could, travelling around by tram and on foot. All of our vehicles had been requisitioned apart from the two we had managed to conceal but which we dare not use openly for fear of losing them too. For reasons difficult now to fathom out, there never seems to have been an attempt to meddle with our house in *Üllöi ut*, with its huge oaken gates secured by robust iron bars. The house seemed to be blessed with amazing luck, avoiding bomb damage and shellfire; one single hit set fire to an area under the ridge of the roof, but thanks to a quick response damage was kept to a minimum. The large well-equipped basement-cum-shelter, which we managed to provide with a sufficient number of the beds from those we had originally acquired for the hospital, was only brought into use on more solemn occasions, in a manner of speaking, when the storm of projectiles raining down upon us from the approaching front line became particularly heavy.

It was on New Year's Day, however, that our turn came. I had called the Nuncio in the morning with the season's greetings, macabre as they were in the circumstances, when the call was interrupted by a shout at the other end: 'A bomb! . . . Every pane of glass in splinters! . . . Bye for now!'

Three hours later on the same day we were sitting together with our extremely hospitable host, Josef Heinrich, and his family in our own room before lunch. Suddenly there was a tremendous bang, with the most frightening crash I'd ever heard, immediately followed by an odd clatter and clink sounding like a shower of huge metal hailstones. All the windows in the building, a hundred or so, were smashed to smithereens and thrown on to the ground outside and into all the rooms. The hostess rushed in, her dark hair glittering with tiny shards of glass.

'Where are the children?' she shrieked desperately.

They were with us, completely unharmed just as we were. Miraculously, the windows in our room had been spared – they faced the courtyard of a neighbouring house which had also escaped damage. Frau Heinrich, moreover, had been standing in her kitchen with her back to the glass door of the pantry. When it was shattered by the blast she therefore avoided getting the sharp splinters in her face and hands. The bomb, it turned out, was a so-called aerial mine with enormous explosive power. There was in fact no other serious damage apart from the loss of window glass, unpleasant enough in the cold of winter. The house owner, however, contrary to what most others had done in the now almost windowless Budapest, had had the forethought to stash away in the cellar all the inside panes of the double glazing, allowing all the rooms soon to be habitable again.

My small apartment situated in a nearby street was hit at about the same time by shellfire which left a huge hole in one of the walls and showered a rain of tiles from the roof over my bed – lucky nobody was sleeping there at that moment. My guest the Colonel I mentioned earlier had just moved! The window frames had held two-metre-high double glazing, and all that was left were a few shards of glass. Water and heating pipes were destroyed, and the furniture was thrown around higgledy-piggledy. We were fortunate in not having to rely on this uninhabitable accommodation, which in any case soon fell victim to roaming marauders. Plenty of these were about, and they spared neither Jew nor Christian as long as there was something to get their hands on.

My wife and I now lived confined to the basement for a whole month. It was trying enough, but we did have a bed each; we had crude and monotonous food to eat, which did however have nutritional value – mostly peas and beans topped up with tomato purée; we had access to water in contrast to many others who were without, and who had to risk their lives fetching it from some well in a courtyard which had survived the bombardment. Tallow candles replaced electric lighting after a couple of days when the current failed, and after we had used up the tiny store of paraffin for our portable tinware lamps. A quick breath of fresh air up in the courtyard was possible from time to time, flexing our muscles by shovelling snow between the almost constant shelling and bombing. A couple of minor fires were extinguished using carbon dioxide spray when it proved too difficult to get water to do the job.

A group of Arrow Cross people paid us a visit late one evening looking for hidden Jews (of whom there were of course quite a number with us). They threatened to blow up the main door if they were not let in, but the labyrinthine passages in the basement were too much for them and all ended well. I was in bed with a cold at that time, and the long white beard I had let grow enabled me to go unrecognised. There would have been an unhappy ending otherwise as I was well-known in Arrow Cross circles after all the commotion I had kicked up. Both my wife and I were wanted as serious criminals for having done our best to save the lives of Jews and other 'malicious' persons. Promises had been made to kill us and our office manager and his wife and children at the first opportunity. Wallenberg's life, too, was seriously in danger, but he was at least for a time protected by his diplomatic status, whereas we Red Cross people were seen now as operating an illegal organisation. The office manager was, however, in the end arrested in the new living quarters to which he had moved after the house he had lived in previously was plundered. He was led away to be sentenced to death, but managed to escape down an alleyway and climb to the attic of a six-storey house where he hid for a couple of days before seeking out a suitable hiding place for himself and his family.

It takes all sorts to make up this world of ours. They include a couple of Arrow Cross people, one of whom did all in his power and at obvious risk for his life to help *us* in our rescue work, making full use of his status within the Party. The other one, armed to the teeth, in one of our protected buildings threatened to shoot my wife if she did not immediately issue letters of protection for forty or so Jews he wanted to rescue. A third one again, of a different type, was captured after the Russian occupation and accused of being behind the murder of some 250 Jews: he indignantly declared that this was an outright lie – according to his own accurate statistics, he had not shot more than 150 . . . Outstanding among the many dreadful crimes committed in the intervals between bombardment and shellfire was the mass murder of over 100 of Wallenberg's Jewish staff, dragged one evening out of the offices where they were living into the street and mown down on the spot. The most ghastly of all must have been the discovery of masses of naked and semi-naked female corpses found in the streets on the Russians' arrival and in a house where they lay . . . beheaded . . .

By the middle of January Malinovsky's advance guard had reached the outskirts of Pest and was approaching the city from a northerly direction, while Tolbuchin's divisions were making their way forward from the south-west on the other side of the Danube, with violent exchanges of fire with the German and Hungarian Arrow Cross regiments. The capital was being threatened from the east, the north and the south.

One day the sky was littered with sheets of paper. In the place of bombs the aircraft poured out a written message, an ultimatum in Hungarian: if the Hungarian military laid down its weapons and the Germans withdrew, every officer and soldier would be treated honourably and Budapest would be spared further destruction. Otherwise they knew who would bear responsibility for the consequences. The same message was carried by two groups of members of parliament who made their way by car under a white flag up to the Buda defence lines. Their proposal for a truce would have saved the beautiful city on the Danube from wanton destruction; it would have been a sensible recognition of the circumstances prevailing as well as a start to constructive negotiations with a Germany which had already lost every prospect of final victory but which was still strong enough to make certain demands for reasonable peace terms. The proposal was rejected out of hand. But that was not all. As the parliamentarians were leaving their car was shot at, resulting in one of the negotiators suffering such serious injuries that he most probably died later. If this was the case, it is no wonder the Russians were furious at this crime against all the accepted rules of warfare which had been in existence since time immemorial, and for which the poor population of our city was to pay the severest penalty. In consequence the struggle continued and our lovely Budapest lay in ruins, and thousands of innocent lives were lost. Still others lost all they owned and were doomed to an existence of hunger and distress.

For now there was no going back. After a couple of weeks Pest had been subjugated by the Russians while Buda was the target for the most devastating shellfire from guns and howitzers. All of the elegant bridges over the Danube were dynamited by the Germans, and each side bombarded the other, day and night, with unremitting intensity, until there was little left standing. Nevertheless, what was perhaps the worst of all was the hand-to-hand fighting, street by street. Barricades were put up in Budapest's radial-shaped streets from all the rubble created by the destruction, while the eternal clatter of machine guns, interspersed with the whine of falling bombs and the shrieks of the dying gave us never a moment of rest or time to think.

When the street battles gradually edged their way towards our building on the interminably long and straight *Üllöi ut,* we firmly believed our time was up. One of the old grandmothers who lived in the building, the widow of a former liberal minister of the old school, and herself a devout Catholic, gathered us all together every evening for a short prayer down in the basement, after which we tried to nestle down in our chilly beds and get to sleep, while outside a tremendous din raged and one wondered if and what one would wake up to.

One evening there was a heavy knock on the walled-up division between our own basement and that of the neighbouring block. Harsh voices uttered something hard to understand.

'Who's there?' we shouted at the tops of our voices in three or four languages. It was difficult to make out the response, but finally we heard:

'*Russkije* . . . .Russians!'

Pick and shovel were put to work, and a few minutes later

the rusty iron door was visible. When it was opened it revealed a score of sweat-stained, dishevelled Russian sappers who one by one crept through the hole.

'Any Germans here?' they quickly asked, brandishing their weapons.

'Not one, thank God,' we said. 'And no Arrow Cross people either. We're all civilians, men, women and children, unarmed, and the building belongs to the Swedish Red Cross. Come and look!'

They made a swift but thorough search and then sat down as a group in the middle of the basement floor. We offered them all tea, which they gladly thanked us for, but refused a meal we also offered them. A couple of them who had minor injuries had their wounds dressed by our doctor, and a while later they fell fast asleep, leaving a single guard in charge of the hand grenades. It had been a long time since we could go to bed with such great relief. My wife, however, stood guard all night. Early the following morning all of our 'guests' had disappeared without having touched a single article among our possessions. They had resumed their peculiar Odyssey from one basement shelter to another.

Concerning the grim scenes played out in other places in the struggle to gain the upper hand, allow me to relate but one example, occurring not far from where we were. The basement of the building where my wife and I had our small flat was occupied by German soldiers mixed in with about 100 terrified tenants who lived there, undoubtedly in the most cramped conditions imaginable. They all had their food and their personal possessions down there in case there was a direct hit from a bomb. After the Russians entered there was an almighty battle which ended with the Russians in command. Before the Germans fled or were captured and wiped out, they had time enough to throw a large hand grenade which set fire to all the timber as well as the stores of food, clothes and money. Five people lost their lives and a number were seriously injured; all of them lost all they had brought with them down into the basement, the contents of which were reduced to a black, smouldering heap of ashes. As luck would have it we were later able to come to the aid of our neighbours, now rendered destitute, with Red Cross relief.

We had already had a series of unpleasant visits – to put it mildly – from the type of marauding gangs which always accompany a victorious army on the march (they stole our wristwatches, of all things) when one day a maintenance unit arrived under the leadership of a particularly discourteous captain and installed its equipment in our courtyard. For fuel, our visitors used what they could find around the house, and some of the rooms were cleaned out of some valuable furniture and left in a deplorable state, though no acts of violence were committed against us. Moreover, our last vehicle, skilfully concealed as it had been, was discovered and removed – we had carelessly failed to provide it with the customary Red Cross markings. This was because it was in actual fact the property of the owner of the house who had placed it at our disposal for as long as we could safely drive through the city – that happy state of affairs belonged to the distant past. We weren't, then, in the best of moods, you might say.

Suddenly a couple of Russian officers in green berets and shoulder straps appeared. They politely made inquiries for me and I was summoned before them.

'Are you Herr Langlet, sir?' they asked. 'Can you read Russian?'

When I had answered in the affirmative, they showed me a type-written sheet of paper and explained:

'Here's a written order from Moscow to place, whatever the circumstances, the ten members of your embassy under our protection. Read it yourself: the list includes your name and your wife's. By pure chance we heard that you could be found here. I'd like you now to decide whether you would prefer to stay in this house or choose other living accommodation. We can provide a guard – four soldiers and a sergeant. They'll be at your personal command day and night.'

I thanked him profusely for his kindness and told the two friendly officers we would rather stay put, having already started to prepare ourselves for a resumption of our activities as soon as circumstances permitted.

The officers turned out to belong to the so-called border *gendarmerie*, a unit directly responsible to the office of the People's Commissariat for Internal Affairs, the NKVD, and they had been assigned to serve with the advance guard of Marshal Malinovsky's army. When they had introduced themselves and I heard that one of them bore the name of Balck, I unconsciously associated it with the now deceased general and leading sporting character we knew as 'Sir Victor' – he had once been my gym teacher at school in Stockholm, and for many years a dear friend of mine.

This Lieutenant Balck turned then to the captain commanding the maintenance corps who, all agape, had been listening to our conversation.

'Comrade', he said in a quiet but determined manner, 'you have twenty minutes to leave this property, and please don't return. Understood?'

The captain, who had strutted around with sword drawn, was now leaning on it. He grew red in the face and spat out:

'How dare you give commands to me, your superior in rank?'

Things were shaping up to a grand old hullabaloo, but the lieutenant kept calm and with a few whispered words got the captain to retire, his tail between his legs, over to the equipment. Exactly eighteen minutes later he drove his unit out through our gateway, and that was the last unwelcome visit we had to our little 'Red Cross fortress', as we later dubbed it.

When we were asked about the location of our embassy and the addresses of the various diplomats and staff, I was unfortunately unable to supply other than a few addresses on the Buda side of the river, and to say that the overwhelming majority of the embassy staff lived on that side.

'I regret, then, that we can do nothing in their respect', was the reply. 'That part of the city, as you must well know, has still not been cleared of Germans. It's still a combat zone, and when it is under the control of the Red Army, there'll probably be another group, not ours, providing you with protection. Is there no other member of the embassy here in Pest?'

Raoul Wallenberg, with whom we had had no contact for weeks, suddenly came to mind, and I recalled it being said that he had moved his office over to the Pest side, though I had no idea where he could be. Fate would dictate that our paths would never cross again. Later on a couple of his colleagues let me know that he had last been seen on 17 January at one of his offices in Pest. One of them claimed that he had intended to try to travel by car to Debrecen where a new Hungarian government had been set up, while the other gave us to understand that he had gone to Malinovsky's headquarters. Still another source maintained that his intent had been to travel into the countryside for a few days' rest after all the trial and tribulation he had been through. Finally we may mention the fact that later in the spring a Hungarian newspaper in a particularly appreciative article concerning his work believed that during the dying days of the Arrow Cross regime a piece of villainy had lured him into a trap and he was abducted to Germany. The true course of events has not yet been ascertained. He may still be alive and emerge unscathed. Since nothing has been heard from him for six months, however, at the time of writing, it is much to be feared that the imperturbably courageous young man has died at his post like a hero. In concluding this chapter I find it fitting to inscribe a simple act of com-memoration – *in gloriam Raoul Wallenberg* – on behalf of the thousands who worship his name and who would with the greatest of pleasure contribute to the setting up of an institution dedicated to preserving the memory of his noble deeds. Many have been honoured with statues for less . . .

THE FOURTH ACT:

The Hungarian Republic

THE Hungarian capital's fate was sealed as we entered the New Year, 1945. Russian armies were in the process of surrounding it on three sides: east, north and south. The Arrow Cross government and its various administrative bodies – to the extent that they had been set up and come into operation – were evacuated towards the west and left Budapest more or less to its inevitable fate as a battlefield between the Germans and the Russians. Wallenberg and the Red Cross continued their relief and rescue work as far as possible in the midst of constant conflict with Arrow Cross gangs and street rabble, who could now give free rein to their violent instincts.

Meanwhile, behind the frontline, far to the east, something entirely new was coming into being: a democratic Hungarian republic had been proclaimed on 21 December in the city of Debrecen. This city, the third largest in Hungary, was not lacking in tradition. It was here the Hungarian Free State had been established under Ludvig Kossuth almost 100 years previously following a vote by a national assembly declaring the Hapsburg imperial family had forfeited the Hungarian crown. On that occasion the new form of government was short-lived. Before the year was out the Hungarian freedom corps had to lay down its arms, crushed between the conspiring military powers of imperial Austria and Tsarist Russia. Now the matter was of a different calibre. The Hungarian freedom movement which had endeavoured to break itself loose from dominance by Hitler's Germany – something we have seen the Regent failed to achieve – now had on its side a new Russia whose triumphant divisions were occupying large swathes of the country.

Debrecen is the very centre of the Calvinist movement in Hungary, followers of the Reformed Church making up approximately one-quarter of the population. The majority of these live in this part of the country, regarding themselves as the most 'genuine' of all Magyars, direct descendants of the Ugrian tribes which more than a thousand years ago wandered into the country from the steppe lands beyond the Carpathian mountains.

In the course of time these people have hardly mixed with Germans, Slavs, Romanians and other nationalities who entered from north, south and west and settled on the plains along the Danube, and still today they are renowned for speaking the purest Hungarian in the entire country. Debrecen is their main religious and political centre, and it was the natural place for a popular movement bent on creating a Hungary free of German influence on democratic lines. Obviously, people there were, as everywhere else, split into different political parties – bourgeois, social democrats, communists – but who nonetheless were fully united in their view that the only possibility of rescuing the nation and rebuilding it lay in breaking with Hitler's Germany and collaborating with the victorious Russians. Delegations from the various parties met and elected, similarly to what they had done in Kossuth's day, a preliminary national assembly with the power to pass resolutions concerning the nation's constitution and governance until such time as peace had been established and a fully legitimate national assembly could take its place following a general election held throughout the country.

This assembly appointed as its president an eminent lawyer, Professor Béla Zsedényi, of the Academy of Law in Miskolc. Negotiations took place in Debrecen with senior officers of the Russian army, which had already occupied the whole of Siebenbürgen and a large part of the Hungarian plateau. A list of ministers was drawn up consisting of representatives of all the democratic parties, including three of the generals who had been present at the Regent's failed attempt in Budapest on 15

October to achieve a break with the Germans and start negotiations with Russia for a truce.

All of these persons, approved of by each of the parties, were summoned to Moscow where Molotov handed over the various portfolios. General Dálnoki-Miklós was appointed Prime Minister, and he led the peace party within the military, managing to remain with some of his troops behind the Russian front which in a series of forced marches was drawing closer to the capital. His family, still in Budapest, miraculously escaped persecution and reprisals and in time were able to be reunited with him. General Vörös was made Minister of War – in his role of Chief of General Staff under the Lakatos government he had countersigned the Proclamation of Truce on October 15, and after a series of adventures succeeded in stealthily passing through the German lines north of Budapest following the *coup d'état* which brought the Arrow Cross regime into power. He was an exceptionally clever and trustworthy man, it must be said, with whom I later established a friendly and confidential relationship. The important post of Minister of Supply was entrusted to General Faragó, who had a full command of Russian having previously been the military attaché in Moscow. I had made his acquaintance in Istanbul in the summer of 1941, when I accompanied the Soviet delegation in Budapest sent home following the outbreak of war between Germany and Russia. Similarly, from Istanbul I accompanied the Hungarian delegation returning from Moscow and headed by the minister Kristóffy. Faragó had then become head of the Hungarian gendarme corps but bore no responsibility for the brutal treatment that had been meted out to the deported Jews. This had been the obnoxious task of a special department set up by First Secretary Baky under the earlier Sztójay regime, and administered by a certain Colonel Ferenczy, who both Wallenberg and I had crossed swords with on a number of occasions in the course of our rescue work.

The bourgeois party group in the new government included Count Géza Teleki. He is the son of the former prime minister who committed suicide rather than be party to the attack on Yugoslavia which Germany forced Hungary to undertake some years earlier. He had himself a few months previously signed a peace treaty which both countries had greeted with full satisfaction and the greatest of optimism. Of the son the following account has been given. When Molotov decreed that he had been appointed Minister of Culture and Education, he replied saying he would only accept the task on condition that his country regained its independence. It appears that the Russian People's Commissar was greatly impressed by this frank and candid response, and changed his order to a friendly request for the Count to be so good as to undertake the task in question. Teleki agreed, as the request must reasonably imply that the condition he imposed would be fulfilled. The fact that he is still at his post would indicate that he has confidence in the pledge given.

On a visit to Debrecen at the beginning of February I got to know most of the remaining ministers, who as a rule represented either the liberal, the social democrat or the communist party, which were generally regarded by the broad base of the population as more or less equal in size and power. Not until the general elections – originally expected to be held in the course of the summer but postponed until 4 November – did the real distribution of votes become clear. A surprisingly large majority gave their vote to the bourgeois block, the so-called 'smallholders party' (nearest equivalent in Sweden the 'folkpartiet') plus the tiny independent democrat party. They obtained 242 seats plus 2 as against the 69+69+23 for the radical left – social democrats, communists and the strongly left-leaning Country Workers' Party. It is therefore probable that a coalition government will be formed of a type similar to the one which emerged about one year ago.

The first task of the government in tackling problems in the near future should then be to establish the definite constitution which at the moment is still provisional, and in accordance with its stipulations appoint a Head of State. Only two names had been put forward as candidates for president prior to my departure from Budapest at the beginning of May. Neither of them – at least at that juncture – had sufficient status to be considered an obvious choice for this high post. One of them was the Nobel Prize-winning Professor Albert Szentgyörgyi, who does of course enjoy a sound reputation in European circles and should be well received by the Anglo-Saxon Big Powers. The other candidate was Count Michael Károly, now well advanced in years, who took power at the request of King Charles in 1918 when the monarchy collapsed, but who very soon afterwards yielded it to the communist Béla Kun. He is rather unpopular in bourgeois circles, and cannot be seen, even if he is approved of by the communists, as a unifying element. This must be even more the case with the current speaker of the parliament Professor Zsedényi, a skilful and flexible politician who, as far as I know, is also in the favour of the Russian powers-that-be, whose authority can be taken as crucial at least at the first presidential election.

All of this was unknown to us, sitting isolated in our Budapest basement until late into the month of January. We were completely cut off from the outside world, and our chances of survival seemed extremely small. Day and night bombs rained down over the unhappy city. Powerful cannon were stationed at every available corner, machine guns rattled uninterruptedly and peppered house façades on all the bigger streets where barricades went up in a rush of enthusiasm. Gangs of Arrow Cross men wreaked havoc everywhere, and it became more and more difficult to intervene and stop their mischief. Any sort of authority was totally absent since the Arrow Cross ministers had fled westwards. Even if such had existed, it would hardly have been any good for us since from December onwards our organisation had been outlawed. Our sole hope was that a Russian victory would soon put an end to a struggle which threatened to remove every brick and stone from a city which had once been so splendid and so beautiful.

We had not the slightest idea of what was being planned in Debrecen. It was as if we were cast away on a desert island, exposed to the fury of the elements and cordoned off from the outside. After the bridges over the Danube had been blown up, we lost all touch with the embassy and with other Swedes in Buda. Neither did we have any contact with Wallenberg and his offices in Pest since if you dared to step out into the street it meant you were a sitting target for goodness knows how many machine guns.

It was, however, a good two weeks before the Russians had gained control of practically the whole of the city east of the river. As the Germans in their desperation had clung on to Buda on the other side, the fighting raged for a long time with undiminished ferocity. From either shore shells and grenades were launched leaving almost every building alongside the quays a smoking ruin, or else fires broke out, and scorched and burnt-out walls were all that remained. Many of the buildings were systematically pillaged by roving gangs of marauders, who grabbed all they could, were often guilty of molesting the womenfolk, and of a totally meaningless destruction of whatever they were either unwilling or incapable of dragging off with them. Apart from the fact that we were almost all of us robbed of our wrist-watches, and that a certain amount of our furniture was used as fuel for the military soup kitchens, on the whole the inhabitants of our Red Cross building survived the devastation fairly well. We did lose our last vehicle and a quantity of clothes and valuables, but in general the Red Cross markings served to protect us from excessive violence as did our gateway, barred as it was with heavy iron girders, even before we were blessed with military protection.

News of what was going on in other parts of the city reached us only sporadically. Checking the truth of the information that was coming in was well-nigh impossible, but some of it you just had to believe, and it was quite plain that hunger and distress prevailed wherever you looked.

After we had acquired our Russian 'green beret' guard enabling us to move about the street in reasonable security, our first big job was to establish some sort of contact with the new authorities as soon as possible. We needed their permission, of course, to carry out the charity work the Arrow Cross had banned.

We encountered no difficulties. The new mayor, Dr Csorba, who had been appointed by a combination of the different party delegates and given the seal of approval by the Russian occupying powers, received me in his office with delightful courtesy, and immediately acknowledged my status as Red Cross delegate as well as the documents referring to the leading members of our staff. One after another they had crept out of their hiding places and, as the constant rain of bullets and grenades declined, ventured out into the snow-covered streets and alleyways strewn with corpses and dead horses.

Armed with these bundles of papers we made our way to the offices of the Russian city commander, General Chernyschov, who represented the Soviet Army's forces in Pest. We were kindly received, and on 2 February he legalised, so to speak, our existence and our operations by stamping our documents and signing them. Furthermore, we were able to introduce to him a number of diplomats who had remained in Pest and represented French, Italian and Greek interests, and who had asked for our assistance, aware that we had a command of the Russian language and were in the Russians' favour. We even succeeded in arranging for a bodyguard for the fairly numerous royalist Italian community; we lodged a young French couple in our quarters, and as far as the Greeks were concerned it appeared they were in no particular danger. Which didn't prevent their minister from causing us more trouble than all the others put together, and with his banter and chatter he wasn't far from exhausting the good-humoured Russian general's patience.

After all these odds and ends had been cleared up, we were visited by the Russian-Belgian Count Tolstoy I have referred to earlier. He produced a document already made out by our ambassador in November authorising him to establish contact with Soviet troops if and when they eventually marched into Budapest. He now wondered whether as I had already established such contact, I wouldn't be offended if he went ahead with the task. It surely seemed a little odd that such an important job should be entrusted to a citizen of a foreign nation – a Belgian – when a national of our own embassy – myself – who had full command of the Russian language was available and would be the natural choice for the job. It was, however, all the same to me since practically all my fellow countrymen were at that time confined to Buda, completely isolated from us, and I would not have been able to do anything for them in any case. Those few Scandinavians who lived on our side of the river, or who had close business connections with Sweden, and were in need of help and support, figured among our clientele anyway and turned to us for assistance.

Tolstoy, then, received my blessing for whatever he wanted to do. He left, and gradually obtained some sort of employment as interpreter and front officer in dealing with foreign citizens' business with the Russian commandant's office. He thereby disappeared from our horizon, and in all probability in time was released from his not so pleasant job in the service of the Russians. The last time I was in touch with him was when one of our 'green berets' asked to see him and I took him along to Tolstoy's office. Tolstoy asked (in German!) how we were getting on at the Red Cross, and I replied in Russian that we were very happy under the protection of our Russian friends, which the Russian confirmed with a charming smile. Our Count was never able to perform any activities on behalf of Swedish interests, equipped though he was with the embassy's authority, and I never subsequently had the pleasure of seeing him again.

The most pressing task for us now was to make contact with the new Hungarian government. We knew next to nothing about it other than it must be situated at Debrecen some 250km from the capital. Getting there appeared to present insuperable difficulties: the railway network was not functioning since the Germans in their flight westwards had torn up all the tracks. No vehicles were available as the last one in our possession, my own little Skoda sporting the Corps Diplomatique plates, had been stolen from under our noses.

Yet Lady Luck was with us once again. One fine day a former member of our staff, Iván Kisházy, an ex-captain attached to the Danube flotilla, appeared at our doorstep and provided us with the welcome news that he had recently been appointed general secretary of the newly organised Hungarian Red Cross and was a sort of right-hand man in Debrecen serving Foreign Minister Vörös. He had been given the assignment of fetching us to take part in a conference with the government. Talk about the right man in the right place at the right time!

That trip crossing the large Hungarian plain was a remarkable experience. A number of the many villages and small towns we passed presented a terrible scene of wanton destruction; others, however, had remained practically undamaged apart from a few shattered windows, and life there seemed to have retained its normal rhythm. During the journey we met or passed Russian vehicles, columns of troops and numerous individuals wandering in both directions, it would seem aimlessly, plodding on under the load of whatever they had been able to retrieve from their burnt-out or ruined homes in different parts of the country.

By midday we had reached a children's holiday camp and tuberculosis clinic which early in the autumn had been opened by our friend the captain on a country estate belonging to László Beökönyi, a Hungarian civil servant working in the Ministry of the Interior and married to a Swedish lady, Märta Bergqvist. The small institution was, it appeared, in the best of health. Our Red Cross markings had been fully respected by the Russian military authorities; food and essential medical supplies were abundant. Both doctor and pharmacist did their job in exemplary fashion so that the local population which had spent time down in their basement shelters could now find remedy for their ailments. Even schoolmistresses were on hand, so that normal education was available for children of all ages. What more could you ask for in a little provincial hole at a time when Germans and Russians were still at one another's throats in the country's capital? It was like a small, safe oasis in the middle of a winter war scenario – the Swedish

Red Cross will long be held in hallowed memory in this little spot, I'm sure! Later in the year we were happily informed that the proprietor of the estate, who had been arrested by the Germans and taken away without our being able to intervene, had survived and was safe in the hands of Allied troops. There was a good chance of his being reunited with his Swedish wife, who meanwhile in the autumn had travelled home with their children and is doing her best here to rouse interest in unhappy Hungary's lot and bring help.

Car trouble forced us to stay the night. The following day there was no way of getting the engine fixed, but the senior officer at the Russian outpost immediately came to our assistance. He loaned us a lorry which was not in use for the moment to tow our car to the distant Debrecen. It was a slow business, but it gave us the opportunity to see more of that part of the country and what had been happening. Road bridges which had been blown up had already been replaced by temporary pontoon bridges. Railway tracks systematically torn up by the retreating German army were being repaired and some sections were already usable. The badly-damaged material that remained after the general destruction was skilfully juggled into useful shape by the handy Russian soldiers so that some sort of rail transport could be achieved.

The last part of the journey took place in a February twilight as we made our way over roads in impossible conditions and the partly-flooded Hortobágy *pusztan* where in happier times as a youth I had enjoyed quite different adventures. The Russian driver's skill in navigating the hazards involved was quite beyond belief. We reached our destination, nonetheless, and it was the Red Cross captain's brilliant idea to seek out the Catholic Dean Bánás who afforded us accommodation in his well-appointed and hospitable home.

For us who had come from the pile of ruins that Budapest had been reduced to, it was a remarkable sensation in Debrecen to find houses and buildings essentially undamaged. Here and there you would see a house that had suffered some damage, but there were none of the huge craters caused by bombs which had disfigured our poor capital, nor the rows of devastated streets. Electric lighting, absent for us for weeks on end, was fully functional, just as was the water supply, which we had sorely missed. Hardly a pane of glass was missing from the windows, and there didn't seem to be a lack of food or fuel. A tasty slice of ham cost all of 15 *pengö*, but it was a slice big enough for two! Just as eye-opening was to see trams running and paperboys selling the papers – in the capital we had had to get used to seeing them disappear.

At nightfall the street lamps went on, and 'curfew' wasn't sounded until 9pm. The local theatre offered performances, and a few cinemas were open, keenly visited by the local people and fraternising Russian soldiers – all of this a sheer novelty for us big-city folk. The large exclusive hotel, *Arany Bika* – the Golden Bull – had been obliged to close its doors following bomb damage, although from the outside it gave no impression of having been hit. All the well-known large hotels in Budapest, however – *Palatinus, Dunapalota, Hungaria, Bristol, Carlton* and *Szent Gellért* down by the river – as well as quite a few in the inner city, stood in ruins with their windows gaping wide and resembling vacant eye-sockets. The scarcity of rooms in Debrecen, where all available hotel rooms were fully booked, turned out to be to our advantage. Our host, I found, was a particularly intelligent man from a well-educated background, and we formed a very warm and lasting friendship, just as I was to do with the Reformed Church Bishop Dr Révész. Both were members of the newly-formed Hungarian Red Cross board and worked in close collaboration with one another. *Here* it was that the common church front I had tried in vain to create in Budapest had been achieved!

All the members of the government greeted us most heartily as very welcome guests. My status as Red Cross delegate was immediately acknowledged by those ministers it concerned, which thereby provided us with a *de facto* legal recognition for our operations. We at once began our collaboration with the Hungarian Red Cross, whose general secretary willingly lent us a hand. His influence with the Minister of Defence, for example, became very clear a little later when the delegate in Hungary of the International Red Cross, Hans Weyermann – to whom we'd offered shelter and hospitality for a few days in Budapest – arrived at Debrecen and asked me to introduce him to the minister. At our audience with General Vörös he was about to present his credentials from his breast pocket when he was stopped by the general with a friendly gesture and the words: 'Anyone coming here with our friend Langlet has no need to identify himself!'

The General gave further proof of his kindness in having sent my own telegrams to Bucharest by personal courier, addressed to the Swedish foreign office with the first news they were to receive about the Swedish community in Budapest. A little later, on the radio, we were able to listen to this communication, broadcast to the entire Swedish nation.

I also had a cordial reunion with General Faragó, who I had last seen in uniform at a reception with our military attaché Lieutenant-Colonel Wester before the latter left for home in the autumn following an air raid which gutted his elegant apartment on the Gellért hillside. The general was now decked out in a shabby black jacket, plus-fours, and aging brown shoes. 'These are the very last clothes in my possession,' he assured us good-humouredly. The Minister of Defence, on the other hand, had a uniform but not a stitch of civilian clothing.

Prime Minister Miklós was fortunate enough to be the owner of a smart dark suit which gave an elegant edge to his trim figure. Serious, calm and collected, with a look in his eyes as firm as his handshake, he gave the impression of a person of remarkable qualities. His position as head of government in a country largely under the occupation of a foreign power while to a lesser degree an unwilling host to the adversary, was of course extremely delicate, demanding a diplomatic stance of considerable discretion. That he was up to the standards demanded of him was borne out by the fact that, despite all predictions to the contrary, he succeeded in maintaining and consolidating his post for almost one year. Later meetings with him served to strengthen impressions of his personality, in which I noticed only one weak spot: he was a passionate collector of stamps, swapping them with child-like delight with my wife, who is a much more modest victim of this innocent psychosis.

We also established agreeable relationships with a number of departmental ministers, principally the highly-gifted Minister of Education and Cultural Affairs, Count Teleki and his charming wife, with the very likable Foreign Minister Dr Gyöngyösi, the Interior, Finance, Health and Justice Ministers, and the social democrat Minister of Industry, Takács. I clinched a deal with the last-named for the manufacture of windowpanes at a factory in the city of Miskolc which belonged to our friend and altruistic Red Cross colleague, Stefan Forgó, who was married to a Swedish woman in our circle of friends. Forgó, an engineer, was perhaps the greatest expert in glass manufacture in Eastern Europe. His life was often in great danger, and he was extremely grateful to us when we came to his rescue.

With his wife and children residing in Sweden, he had every right to claim Swedish citizenship, which he never managed to acquire, despite other people with far more tenuous claims succeeding. The reasons behind the rejection of his applications remain a perfect mystery for those of us who were out there in the thick of things.

Forgó's life hung by a thread for weeks and weeks – a special providence, it seemed, kept him alive. When he was prevented from coming to Sweden and suffered all manner of terrible experiences in surviving in his native land, his tremendous energy and talent were to benefit his country. I have recently read in the press that his glassworks have succeeded in supplying the capital with a sizable quantity of window panes which are going to be such a godsend in the coming winter months. Budapest will thus have our country to thank for its refusal to accept him.

Sadly, in a similar case, the consequences were quite the reverse. Another Hungarian of Jewish descent, Dr Georg Benes, who was also married to a Swedish woman in full possession of her citizenship, suffered the same inexplicable rejection. He too, like Forgó, was one of our colleagues in the Red Cross, and was saved from Arrow Cross harassment. The house where he was working was hit by a bomb during the heaviest fighting and was partly demolished. Helping a badly-injured colleague to escape the burning building where they were sheltering, he himself fell victim to the bombardment and his charred body was later found among the ruins. One of many human tragedies played out among the chaos and havoc, plainly avoidable if bureaucratic red tape had only been tied up with a little heartfelt compassion and understanding. Bureaucracy appeared not to have stood in the way of the clearly unwarranted issue of a number of passports for individuals not deserving them, among them a notorious scoundrel whose case will subsequently be examined.

Perhaps the most important benefit of our trip to Debrecen, I am inclined to suggest, has been the acquaintance of two of the new democracy's most influential men. One of them was the Communist Party chairman, Mátyás Rákosi, who had been described to me as an extremely inaccessible and rather hard-boiled fellow. Gaining admittance to his office was not easy. At the door stood a young militiaman duly armed with a pistol, who let me in after permission had been obtained from a guard post heavily manned by policemen. From here a call was made to the secretariat, which responded regretting that Herr Rákosi was not available. The same procedure was repeated for the next couple of days until I was lucky enough to get my man on the other end of the line, whereupon with the greatest friendliness he burst out:

'Well, is it you? So nice for us to meet! Excuse my lack of courtesy in having you come to no avail, but I've been so busy with meetings recently that my secretary has been saying no to all visitors. I'm on my own just now, so if you like come straight up and we'll have a chat.'

The much-discussed communist leader turned out to be quite the reverse of what had been said of him. A rotund and talkative man with an easy-going nature, a charming personality in his simple and natural way, he was well-educated and had a good command of languages as well as a genuine concern for social issues, and he evidently possessed an open mind towards political convictions other than his own. Although he was clearly aware of my own bourgeois tendencies, we immediately found common ground in our interest for social welfare involving the entire community. It wasn't my fault that the ten-minute talk I had requested and was ready to restrict myself to turned into an hour and a half of intense conversation.

After a few very complimentary words about our Red Cross work – of which he appeared to be very well-informed – he suddenly threw the question at me:

'But why have you chosen to come and see just *me*, situated as I am outside official circles in this country?'

'In the first place,' I replied, 'because I read your last public statement in the press, and it coincides in many respects with my own somewhat unpretentious ideas on social reforms for Hungary, whose development and evolution I've been familiar with for the last fifty years. But most of all, because you are, or will be, the most powerful person in the Republic of Hungary, and I would hope to gain your favour for our work at the Swedish Red Cross.'

'You already have it,' was his reply. 'But I think you mistake the breadth and depth of our party's influence in matters of state. We do not make up a majority of the population in any way, and any success we may reap in presenting our ideas is entirely dependent on co-operation with other groups of opinion. As you know, there are five parties all in all, of which the three largest – small farmers, social democrats and communists – are more or less equal in strength. We communists don't have the slightest chance of coming out on top, at least in a foreseeable future.'

'You don't think Hungary is going to be made a Soviet state,' I rejoined, 'based on communist principles on a Russian pattern, putting the leadership in your hands as chairman of the party? I've been led to understand that the present set-up is only provisional, and that it'll soon be replaced by a one-party government under your leadership.'

'Absolutely not. At least that'll take a long time, and we'll have to be content with trying to put through what we consider the most important policies for the moment – and that is wiping out poverty and seeing that, as is the case in your own country, each and everyone can enjoy a modest but decent livelihood. Nobody must starve to death or be without the essentials of subsistence. Food, clothes and living accommodation for all, care for the sick, while small, abandoned children must not be allowed to perish for want of care. Our most immediate concern should be to withstand a possible menacing reaction of the type that prevailed at the end of the First World War, and to get the other political parties to join us in pursuing social reform.'

This was entirely correct, and our opinions coincided on many issues, even though the general political viewpoint differed. On his travels Rákosi had also been in our country and praised our quiet but swift progress along the path of social welfare towards cultural and material prosperity. He eagerly asked after the friends he had acquired in Sweden, and received such information as I was able to supply him with.

'We've decades of negligence on the social front to make good,' were his last words, 'and we are going to have to struggle hard to create the groundwork necessary for developing along lines similar to those you have chosen in your own country.'

We parted the best of friends, and he was kind enough to promise his assistance for our return to Budapest in one of the very few vehicles available.

I finally had to refuse his friendly offer since the matter was resolved in another way, particularly helpful to our continued activity serving the Red Cross, when the following day I paid a visit to Professor Béla Zsedényi, provisional President of the National Assembly, and thus for the time being the leading figure in the new government. I found him to be a man of great intelligence, not to say wisdom, and his behaviour combined exceptional political discretion with a sense of calm dignity. Similarly to Rákosi, he expressed his high appreci- ation of the work we had so far been performing, and assured me without reservation that every assistance would be lent us in the future. He also promised to recommend us warmly to Marshal Voroshilov, who was in Debrecen at that moment and with whom he had a pleasant relationship. On top of everything he was kind enough to offer me a lift in his car back to the capital, an offer I obviously accepted with the greatest gratitude.

It was a much more pleasant ride back than the trip out had been, and more rewarding. We made a detour to the north-east and visited the city of Nyiregyháza, somewhere I had never been before and which was happily untouched by the ravages of war. We had a meeting with the president's fellow party member, the Protestant Túróczi, bishop of the East Hungarian diocese, a sagely distinguished gentleman who received his Swedish guest with open arms. He beseeched me to seek help in my country to aid the sister church in Hungary which in a number of places had suffered heavy losses owing to bombing and the warring parties' cross-fire, to say nothing of the rest.

A similar request was made by the administrative officers of the Protestant church in Budapest, estimating rebuilding costs at several million Swedish *kronor*, a sum it was hoped to obtain in the form of a loan from the Swedish state. Without com- mitting myself to any prospect of success, I promised to forward the request to the extent it might have any effect in our prosperous country. I haven't been given any high hopes, but it is at least certain that the Hungarian Protestant church has a keen advocate in the person of none other than our own outstanding bishop who, as with his never-to-be-forgotten predecessor, Nathan Söderblom, seems to be here, there and everywhere! There's no question he will do all in his power to help. From Nyiregyháza the journey continued to Tokay and Miskolc, places I knew from a long time ago. A radiant February sun shone down over vast fields of snow, and over brownish meadows, only half of which had been ploughed. Here and there a green patch of earth showed a tender crop of winter wheat, which in normal times would have covered half of the area, and which was an ominous sign of impending famine – the harvest would have to be virtually insignificant. The population in what under normal circumstances was a grain-exporting country was going to go hungry, perhaps starve to death, if relief did not arrive soon from abroad.

The flat countryside around the famous Tokay plateau of vineyards lay mostly under water. We had to cross the river nearby along a seemingly endless timber bridge erected by the Russian army to replace the noble iron construction dynamited by the retreating Germans, the debris of which had blocked the river and converted the fields around into an inland lake. On the other side of the plateau we could see how field after field had turned a dull brown colour where the sugar beets could not be harvested in the midst of the fierce fighting but had to be left to rot in the ground. The big sugar factory at Szerencs where we made a detour was virtually undamaged, but as a result of the extreme scarcity of raw materials found itself obliged to produce toffees for the Russian army and cardboard boxes for cigarettes. One advantage of this was that quite a few men and women were given employment, though on the other hand the factory has failed to make any notable contribution to the huge demands for sugar in what has always been an essentially sugar-producing country.

Potatoes and cabbage, too, had only been partially harvested; whole fields of vegetables were full of them, frozen in the ground. It was heart-rending to see the wanton destruction caused by people in conflict who really speaking had little to quarrel with each other about, but who, as a result of the madness of a criminal sadist, were constrained to go about killing, burning and destroying everything they came across.

In the city of Miskolc I was given the opportunity to get involved in the business of the manufacture of glass for windows. It was, of course, a matter of extreme urgency for the suffering capital city, where practically every building, including those which had not otherwise been damaged, showed a mosaic of gaping holes where the windows had been, in some cases boarded up with planks nailed to the frames. In point of fact, I was delighted that our engineer Forgó was *not* allowed entry into Sweden, for it was he who was able to serve his own country in a field in which hardly anyone else could replace him. Fortunately there remained a large amount of undamaged machinery in his factory, while supervisors and specialists were eagerly awaiting the arrival of raw material for production to begin. On reaching Budapest I found Forgó very happy with the news, and he immediately made arrangements for glass manufacture to begin, a welcome initiative making life a little easier for the good citizens of the capital.

In spite of the insufferable bottlenecks caused by marching soldiers, Russian military vehicles and unhappy souls wandering aimlessly through the streets and along the roads, we reached our destination as night fell, penetrating the suburbs of a still largely blacked-out Budapest, eager to find out what had been happening during our two-week absence. Fighting in the terribly-devastated Buda part of the city was not yet over. Street battles continued, the grim details of which almost defy description, and which we otherwise only got to know about through hearsay.

On the other hand, however, there were some pleasant surprises in store for us at our Red Cross office. It turned out that our new office manager, an exceptionally inventive lawyer full of initiative, Dr L. Josefovits, had succeeded in obtaining both food and medicine in quite large quantities. Half-a-dozen soup kitchens were already in full working order. Our own little cottage hospital was filled with patients, and had an additional annexe close by; ten or so different hospitals enjoyed our support and kept a workforce, employed by us, busy.

A fair number of our friends, who we scarcely dared hope to see again, turned up and gave us a warm welcome. These included the embassy attaché Lars Berg, who had trusted to luck and defying the crossfire rowed himself over the Danube in a boat and was now lodged with us together with a Jewish secretary and two female assistants – a rather questionable staff situation for an embassy not yet recognised by the new regime. I was told that he wanted to requisition our 'green beret' guards and our flag for his own embassy office, but I let it be known that the guard had been specially allotted to me personally and assigned to the building I had chosen as home for myself and my wife. Naturally we offered the young man and his companions both living quarters and office premises, as well as feeding them from our Red Cross kitchen. We were thus able to make do with what we had, and our communal life proceeded quite well for the month we were together without any friction other than when I had to put my foot down and ban an excessive amount of gambling in our premises.

Berg had quite a long account to give of a number of incidents which took place at the embassy building, about which I later received a variety of reports. I'd rather refrain here from relating them since no member of our organisation has had the opportunity to testify to the acts of plunder and assault that took place. The main thing, however, was that according to Berg's account – which would later prove to be fully correct – every member of the embassy staff and of the Swedish community on the Buda side of the river was alive and in reasonable health, a fact I was able to report at the first opportunity to our Foreign Office via Debrecen and Bucharest. The members of the staff had stayed at the embassy building the whole time together with quite a large number of guests who had sought refuge there, and all of them had had to suffer a series of nasty incidents which ended in most of the articles and fixtures of any value being carted off. The ambassador had been given accommodation in the bomb-proof cellars of my friend Count Esterházy up at the 'Castle'. The Swiss embassy was housed there too, having acquired the place as offices after our own embassy had declined a similar offer. Ekmark, Anger and Carlsson, as well as Ms Nilsson and von Bayer and his wife, together with our very close friends Langhard the agronomist and his son and Lundmark the businessman and his young wife – they had been married in the autumn in a Catholic church on the Buda side – all of them appeared to have found shelter of some kind at some place or other, and all were said to be alive and well.

To start with, the immediate question we had to deal with was how to get our embassy boss over to our safe house in Pest as soon as possible. Berg, a man of great courage, straightaway offered to row back over the river to fetch him – our 'green berets' forbade me from risking such an adventure since they were personally responsible for my life and well-being. I wasn't exactly in the prime of youth, either, as well as having a fairly heavy cold after the various hardships endured during the Debrecen trip. Young Berg, on the other hand, was just that . . . young, strong, willing and able.

And so it was. He set off on his expedition, only to return in the evening, all alone and quite down in the dumps, his mission incomplete. The ambassador had refused our offer of a place of safety as long as his two colleagues, the Papal Nuncio and the Turkish minister, remained behind in a dangerous situation. The little rowing boat was faced with the impossible task of transporting both of these fairly rotund gentlemen as well.

There seemed to be no easy way out. My wife suggested seeking the help of our Russian friends, the 'green berets'. An officer appeared immediately but explained that he had no authority to act on the Buda side of the river, only on our Pest side. After a great deal of persuasion, however, he agreed (it would be entirely our responsibility) to let us go and fetch our ambassador, and as soon as we had him safely in our offices, he would be entitled to the same shelter and protection as ourselves. He finally went as far as allowing us to borrow a farmer's hay wagon with a soldier driving and a guard. A new pontoon bridge had been built some way up the river and we could reach the castle on the other side if luck was on our side and if the German front – as it was being said – had been pushed back up onto the high hills behind Buda.

Unfortunately, another couple of days had to pass before everything had been arranged and suitable living quarters made shipshape for our distinguished guests in what was now a rather overcrowded Red Cross building. When the expedition, after something like a 50km detour which included a visit to the old embassy building, did return in the evening, it was to provide us with the following information. The very day before, the ambassador had been picked up by a Russian convoy belonging to Tolbuchin's army and taken, together with the embassy's Hungarian chancery officer, to Dunavecse, in the far south of Hungary. Other embassy staff members were probably there, too, or would be moved there very soon.

Fate, then, had intervened and we were one day late despite our good intentions. As far as the representatives of the Vatican and Turkey were concerned, they would only have been able to come over to us in their capacity as friends and guests of our ambassador, even if they had been found, which they weren't. Archbishop Rotta's exact whereabouts were unknown – nevertheless, in time he was rescued and sent on an evacuation train to Italy together with Monsignore Verolino. The Turkish embassy lay in ruins. Later we learned to our immense dismay that our very dear friend, Mme Kállay, the former prime minister's charming wife, had been fatally hit by shrapnel in the middle of a conversation with a visitor, and her funeral had later taken place. Her husband, as we mentioned earlier, had fled there after the 19 March coup together with his family, and benefited from its extraterritorial immunity.

During the autumn I had paid them a visit on a number of occasions. When in December the government decided to leave the capital, however, and an ensuing state of anarchy reigned, the embassy building appears to have been stormed by an Arrow Cross mob demanding the surrender of Kállay; otherwise the building would be set on fire. In order to protect his wife and his hosts Kállay's truly chivalrous action was to step outside of his own accord and place himself in the hands of his enemies. It then seems he was immediately transferred to Germany, where remarkably enough he was later found by Allied forces and rescued. According to reports he is now living on the island of Capri. It is fervently to be hoped that this intelligent and well-disposed statesman may be repatriated to serve his country, which unquestionably suffered a huge loss when he was prematurely removed from his post.

More or less simultaneously with our unsuccessful attempt to bring our ambassador over to Pest, members of the new Hungarian government began to move to the capital from their temporary base in Debrecen. Some of them were able to take up office in their respective ministerial buildings, inasmuch as they were situated in Pest and had been spared the general devastation. The prime minister's offices in the handsome Austro-Hungarian Imperial palace having been destroyed, he was installed in the premises of the huge National Commercial Bank. Similar measures were taken for other ministries which had had their buildings reduced to rubble following the German withdrawal on the Buda side. The Speaker of the National Assembly, for instance, was able to take his place quite comfortably in the vast, noble parliamentary edifice erected in neo-Gothic style at the turn of the century. On my visits to see him I was able to confirm the fact that the building had not suffered any important damage other than the proud and lofty dome having been shot through.

We maintained our excellent connections with other ministries as well in expectation of the financial assistance from home promised us by the Central Committee of the Red Cross in Stockholm, but which was still not forthcoming. Under the circumstances this aid was of the most urgent necessity, and would have enabled us to expand our work. There was, admittedly, no postal service in operation between Sweden and Hungary, but it was known through my messages via Bucharest that I was in constant touch with our vigorous and exceptionally accommodating embassy there, which in turn always found ways to reach us after communications had finally been established through the offices of a Hungarian government courier.

Towards the end of February there was an incident which might well have ended very unhappily for us, but which in point of fact took a more propitious turn. Owing to an oversight on the part of our caretaker, who neglected to report

149

the matter to our 'green berets', a Russian officer bearing the insignia of the political division was allowed to enter. Our guards would in the normal way quite simply have slammed the door in the face of the political officer, as they did with whoever lacked the authority to enter, regardless of his rank and position. His mission was to enquire about a letter we had despatched to his superior on the express and urgent request of one of Wallenberg's secretaries. The latter had claimed it was the only way to save the life of a colleague since Wallenberg himself, according to his report, had left for Marshal Malinovsky's headquarters and was unable to intervene – it should, he meant, be our plain duty to do everything we could in Wallenberg's place. It was difficult to say no, and the letter was typed out on our Russian-language typewriter and sent off to the appropriate headquarters.

The Russian officer wanted now to check that the letter came from us; he checked the typing and found it tallied. He subsequently invited us politely to accompany him in his car 'for a friendly chat' – 'po dusjam' as they say in Russian. We could have refused and summoned our 'green berets', who doubtless would have been on the spot in no time and shown the officer to the door. But our consciences were clear, and we didn't want to say no and thereby perhaps provoke unjustified suspicions.

We therefore went along and on arrival were shown into a room where several other persons were waiting to be admitted to the commandant's office. Time dragged on, but we were treated to a plentiful and much better meal than we had been eating for weeks at home, where the variety of food generally consisted in having peas one day and beans the next. Several hours went by before the turn came for us to be grilled, as we thought, by a major and his two assistants who seemed to be eager to put us through our paces. Our documents were produced and found to be entirely satisfactory. Our identity cards stamped and signed by General Chernyskov stood us in good stead, in addition to the fact that we had both mastered the language and were in no need of the usual interpreter, who might well make a bit of a mess of things.

When all preliminaries were over and we were personally declared bona fide, the major approached the issue which had brought us there – the letter referring to Wallenberg's colleague. Where was this Wallenberg, where did he live, and why was he hiding? He was probably a German, by the sound of the name.

In reply to the first question we could only offer what it said in the letter – that Wallenberg, in the words of the secretary, had travelled east, to the headquarters. We hadn't heard from him for several weeks, and had not the slightest idea where he could be living.

'Then you shouldn't have written what you did, as you didn't know whether it was true!' was the remark from the major.

It should be freely admitted that we did indeed have our doubts in allowing the letter to be written, but let ourselves be persuaded. The fact that the Wallenberg family was not German but just as Swedish as I was, resident in Sweden for at least the last couple of hundred years, this I could draw on history to prove.

'But you Swedes are all friends of the Germans, aren't you?'

'Politically, as you know, we are strictly neutral. Individually, anyone can think what he will, and I myself was a warm admirer of the *old* Germany. But let me say this much: we're practically all enemies of Hitler, with some very, very few exceptions. Is that all you need to know?'

The major appeared to be satisfied and, nodding to his two assistants, explained that they did not need to go any further, and were there any questions or requests from our side?

We exchanged glances with each other as much as to imply that now was the opportunity, if we watched our step and acted carefully, and we began to make a list:

- to continue our activities, unhindered, for charitable ends;
- to count on a modicum of appreciation and full inviolability for the members of our staff;

- to dispose of a number of passenger vehicles and lorries indispensable for our work, in addition to a supply of petrol essential for transporting commodities to starving children out in the countryside so that they could fill themselves on bread, milk and fattening substances, and for the transport back of food for the starving population of the capital.

The major gave the impression of finding all of this quite reasonable, and was perhaps pleasantly surprised by our not having particular requests for ourselves, only for our *protégés*. His response, in any case, was quite friendly:

'All of this you can be sure of receiving in time, but for the moment you'll have to have a bit of patience until this city gets a little more settled, and this may take quite a while, I fear.'

We were driven back home, very courteously, by a captain whose orders were to see we reached our living quarters safe and sound. It was a pretty grim trip along snow-covered streets littered with heaps of debris through the darkness of the night, the only light visible coming from the glow of entire rows of burning buildings. Everything was fine with us, however, until we reached our gateway where Sergeant Dimitry, in charge of our 'green beret' guard, was on the brink of total despair wondering what had kept us so long and what could have happened to his careless 'professor' and his wife. He didn't mince his words in mercilessly scolding the completely innocent captain – who, incidentally was not the same one who had driven us off to the interview earlier in the day! He did, however, give us a hearty embrace in his sheer joy at seeing us back home unharmed, but quarrelled with us for not having used his own soldiers as an escort when we left with the first captain, who could have been any old rascal!

'There are a lot of Germans and Arrow Cross louts who've got hold of a Russian uniform and learnt broken Russian,' he said. 'If you'd been kidnapped, all five of us here would have been shot at dawn for failing to keep a proper eye on you. Promise me now this mad act will never be repeated. Just imagine, going off with the first blasted clown who managed to squirm his way into this building. It's still not properly safe here yet. Just today we bumped off a couple of Germans who were shooting at our people from a window, and up there in the museum attic opposite us there are probably four more of them we'll have to take a pot-shot at tomorrow morning . . . '

With that, our little adventure was over. We felt satisfied to have toed the line and not refused to accompany the Russian officer for the interview with the major, whatever the risks involved. Thus we had been presented with a golden opportunity – while surviving the ordeal – of getting into the good books of the Russian political police. It might be a useful resource to have for the future.

And so it was. Our relations with the Russian occupying power subsequently suffered no problems. Quite the reverse. We were able to retain our 'green berets' for a further couple of months, and under their protection our work proceeded undisturbed. We were even able to count on their assistance when on occasion we undertook a task not strictly speaking within our field of action. Nobody could force themselves into our building against our will – as long as we needed an escort out in the street a Russian soldier was always available. The meagre quantity of food we had succeeded in storing away was never the target of looting, while the ancient lorry our office manager had got hold of – and which was the only one available – was able to commute between the starving capital and a couple of places in the south of Hungary where certain commodities could be procured, admittedly at a high cost.

Our tiny hospital, situated on the ground floor of the building, served the sick and wounded as far as space permitted, and Russian soldiers were sometimes treated and given help. A sick bay was set up on the opposite side of the street in the Museum of Arts and Crafts, now cleared of snipers. The Red Cross sign and flag were a firm guarantee for the safety of the museum collection: the only way in was through the same gateway that led to the improvised sick bay. Other hospitals in dire need of provisions were supplied by us

with food and medicines. The same applied to a Russian field
hospital which had been damaged by the shelling and had part
of its equipment destroyed. The soup kitchens the city
gradually succeeded in setting up also operated under our
administration. Some members of the Scandinavian community lived with us at times; others called in on a regular
basis and collected food, while others who had lost the greater
part of their belongings received financial help in exchange for
a pledge to reimburse us when they could, either through
assistance from the state or from their own assets back in their
home country.

The biggest difficulty we were up against, however, was
really the lack of transport facilities. All the tramway lines were
out of order; the overhead wires had been shot to pieces in the
constant exchange of fire, the electric powerplant was unable to
provide current for a long period of time, and most of the trams
were unserviceable anyway. There was a chronic shortage of
cars; my own little CD-marked car had finally been discovered
in its cleverly-concealed spot and removed, and when I
reclaimed it from the person who had 'borrowed' it, I was met
with a friendly smile and a shrug of the shoulders:

'Have you forgotten there's a war on still? Some lose their
heads, others lose their cars. You want to count yourself lucky
you still have your head, and console yourself that it's only the
car you've lost . . . !'

We managed to track down an old cart and a couple of small
emaciated horses. I made a few essential trips on the cart, and
even on one occasion gave the Speaker of the National
Assembly a lift after his car had been stolen. We hardly had
enough fodder for our poor little dobbins, so we sent the cart
out into the countryside to scrape together some hay and oats,
and that was the last we saw of our carriage-and-pair . . .

Borrowing a car from one of the ministries which gradually
moved from Debrecen into the capital would not have involved
too much trouble if only they had had one to spare. This was
hardly possible, however, as the Foreign Ministry, for example,
had a mere two at their disposal – one for the Foreign Minister

and his deputy, and the other one for all the other ministry officials! There was, therefore, nothing for it but to walk – a bit of a job as the distances were long and required a lot of time in view of the many clients we had, requesting help and advice from the only office we had been able to set up for the moment. Visiting friends and acquaintances in need, or even finding out whether they were still alive, under these circumstances was hardly possible.

We were living hand-to-mouth and were forced to restrict ourselves to helping those who came to us, already a good many people. Almost daily we received a visit from someone we had had few hopes of ever seeing again alive, and our joy was naturally overwhelming. On other occasions, however, we received the sad news of loyal and close friends who had lost their lives in air raids or exchanges of fire, or whose bodies had been dug out of the ruins of a building that had collapsed or had been gutted by fire. The dead were generally buried in the nearest park or garden with a cross or a piece of wood on the grave and a pencilled name – if the identity was known. When an undertaker was not available, I would sometimes act the part and read a simple prayer for the deceased, so that his or her kith and kin would at least be spared the ignominy of seeing the corpse stuffed into the earth without ceremony as if it were a dead animal being buried.

The mangled corpses of horses lay here and there along the streets of Budapest, and as long as the winter weather raged starving people would surface and carve themselves off a slice of meat. What remained of these carcasses together with all the debris resulting from gutted houses and vehicles, and carts, carriages and smashed furniture, were gradually gathered up and loaded on to railway wagons. Tramway tracks were cleared and an ancient locomotive hauled the stuff away with many a shrill whistle and warning bell. For a long time a number of city squares, riverside quays and other important public places were strewn with huge stinking rubbish heaps sometimes five or six feet high. Wooden beams and other items of timber fallen down into the street were often a godsend for those people who needed some sort of fuel to heat their windowless homes – a shortage of bedclothes and blankets contributed to the trials and tribulations most people were enduring. Even on the Pest side of the river, where most of the apartment buildings were in fairly good shape, life presented such a long series of problems that you wondered how people could put up with the misery. We ourselves were fortunate enough to be in a better position than most and were able to go on with our relief work, thanks in part to the fact that our Red Cross headquarters by a freak of fate had practically escaped damage, and also in part to our landlord's wise decision to keep the inner panes of glass in reserve when the outer ones were smashed.

While our central office, then, to the best of its abilities tried to succour the needy, a few of our colleagues who had been cut off from us during the fiercest fighting set up a couple of valuable branch offices. One of them, situated in a distant suburb of the city called Ujpest, was managed with considerable success by our chief secretary, helped by a number of competent young people. In the face of constant risk and danger he had managed to escape the Arrow Cross mobs, who had looted his home and threatened to murder him, his wife and their two small children. He emerged from his hiding place in Ujpest, quickly established excellent relations with the local authorities, and set up a hospital, soup kitchen, orphanage and other institutions. He appears to have organised everything exceptionally well, with a minimum of assistance on our part, but in the end was gradually incorporated in the reorganised Ministry of Industry and was forced to leave its management in other hands. Owing to our lack of communications it wasn't until later on that we were able to be fully connected with this branch and link it up to our central activities.

The other branch, a larger and more comprehensive one, had been founded in the city of Pécs in southern Hungary by the lecturer in Swedish there, Dr Márton Vörös, who for many years had been in charge of Swedish academic matters, and who had accompanied me on my 1,000km horseback ride through Hungary in the summer of 1931. He now occupied the post of keeper of the city archives in Pécs and came to play an important role in the city following the Soviet occupation. As long as fighting continued in the vast area around Lake Balaton between Pécs and Budapest, there was no hope of getting in touch with him, and even after the Germans had been driven away it was only possible by means of a temporary courier owing to the ruinous state of the railway line. His reports on the measures that had been taken and on the requirement for financial support did not arrive until late in the spring, by which time in accordance with an order from Stockholm Swedish Red Cross operations had been discontinued. We informed him, of course, as soon as we could, and invited the branch office to be incorporated in the newly-formed Swedish–Hungarian Society. To the extent that this society in future can benefit from support from Sweden, operations in Pécs will naturally also be included.

One day in the middle of March, as I was recovering from a rather nasty bronchial upset following a heavy cold, and was for the moment bed-ridden, we were treated to a huge surprise. Somebody came rushing into the room shouting:

'The Swedish ambassador Danielsson is here!'

Sure enough, he had arrived by car from the internment camp at Dunavecse together with Anger and Ekmark in the custody of a Russian gendarme unit – but not the one our 'green beret' boys belonged to, which was under Tolbuchin's command. We were overjoyed to see each other again. What, then, had happened in the meantime, and what would happen now?

The news we were told was quite sensational. The entire embassy would be leaving Hungary in a day or two for Bucharest – some of the way by lorry, according to reports, as the rail link was not yet fully restored – and from there on home via Moscow and Finland. The idea was to allow those who had been interned in Dunavecse to pick up their belongings in Budapest, from where we would all make the journey together back to Dunavecse for onward transport to Bucharest.

This arrangement would include Berg, who had been living with us for a month; Ms Bauer, our guest for no more than a few days, and Ms Nilsson, who we hadn't seen for several months. Two more persons from the embassy staff, Carlsson and Mezey, and – if my memory doesn't fail me – Marghel who was employed in the so-called B department tending to Argentinian affairs, were waiting in Dunavecse where the journey would commence. Arrangements concerning me and my wife were of another nature. We were dependent on our 'green beret' gendarmes attached to Malinovsky's army, and were only allowed to leave Budapest after instructions from them. Added to which was the not-to-be-ignored circumstance that doctor's orders were to remain in bed for a few more days to avoid contracting pneumonia in the late winter chill.

An agreement was reached for us to join the convoy at a later date: when all was said and done a start would not be made from the internment camp for at least a week or so.

'How are things for our people over at the internment camp?' I asked one of the Russian officers who had come from there.

'Splendid!' he replied. 'They're sitting in a golden cage, have very nice rooms, and are eating heartily. As you see, they've already made a remarkable recovery from their hardships living underground in the cellars of Buda!'

The reason for the exodus from Budapest was twofold. Partly consideration for their personal safety in view of the roving bands of hooligans it was still difficult to do anything about, and partly – and this must of course have been the principal motive since we who were living in complete safety were also included – because of an order issued to the effect that all foreign members of embassies belonging to neutral states were to leave Hungary. As long as the new democratic regime was not recognised by their respective governments, diplomatic representation in Hungary had no meaning. Not until normal conditions had been restored, peace declared and a Head of State elected could either a Swedish or any other diplomatic representative be furnished with credentials and resume their work.

This did make a fair amount of sense, although it was indeed odd that members of other embassies still remained in the city – some on our side of the river, in Pest, and some, as we learned later, in Buda. Nobody was able to explain why there was such a hurry for the Swedes to leave.

We saw nothing of our compatriots in the course of the day until they returned in the evening together with Ms Nilsson, who had been fetched from her home. Nightfall prevented their departure, and consequently we had six guests spending the night in our house – or rather seven, as a Russian guard officer with a beautiful command of French who served as an interpreter for his commander had to be given lodging together with the Swedish gentlemen, and had his bed placed next to the ambassador's. We did what we could to take into consideration Ms Nilsson's age and circumstances: this included her first real hot bath for weeks, which put her in the best of moods. She didn't have a word to say about her own activities which had been separate from our own Red Cross relief work, which is why we assume she had wound up the activity.

A SWEDISH FINALE

EARLY in the morning of 15 March – traditionally National Day in Hungary, which had still been celebrated the year before with the usual festivities – our guests left our home for their temporary port of call, some 80km south of Budapest. The departure gave rise to some heated arguments with our 'green berets', who would not let anyone leave our house without express orders from their commander, even threatening to shoot. Finally one of their officers was summoned, and he gave permission to the members of the embassy staff and their Russian escort to leave, strictly 'on their own responsibility'. We ourselves were urged, by the Tolbuchin military convoy, to be prepared to be picked up on 19 March – this happened to be the anniversary of the first German coup against the legal Hungarian government under Kállay, who was now a prisoner in Germany. As for them turning up on that day, we'll believe it, we thought, when we see it! As we were under Malinovsky's command, we couldn't take orders from the other side of the Danube. In response to our query to our 'green beret' guard we were brashly told:

'You won't receive permission to leave Budapest until *we've* got the necessary orders from Moscow. Our duty is to protect you, and you're to stay here and not worry yourselves about anything until fresh instructions come through!'

The upshot of it all was that we continued with our Red Cross work, and in the end nobody from the internment camp came to fetch us. We did, however, have to deal with a number of other problems during this final period. Fate would have it that we were prevented from seeing our homeward-bound fellow-countrymen again, while matters concerning the affairs of the Swedish embassy were to give us a number of headaches over the next couple of months.

Before he left, the ambassador had entrusted my wife with a couple of tasks, one of which was simple enough to perform and was immediately carried out. She was to request of a British citizen, namely the Mr Dickinson referred to earlier, that he take charge of the now-abandoned embassy building. He refused, however, although for very convincing reasons (which need not be gone into here), and wrote down his refusal and the reasons for it after I had expressly requested an unambiguous reply.

My wife's other task was considerably more intricate and in equal measure – at least in my opinion – unreasonable. It involved collecting from the embassy building a large number of packages containing expensive deposits stored away in a safe built into a dining-room wall, which the ambassador had given orders to have blown open as its keys for some reason had got lost. We were then to bring the packages with us to Bucharest (where we supposedly would be going within a few days) to be delivered to him there for transport on to Stockholm. Why? we wondered. To me it was utterly incomprehensible since most of the deposits belonged to people resident in Budapest who would surely want to have access *there* to their belongings. Which in point of fact turned out to be the case.

There was a third task given by the attaché Berg, but fortunately not to us but to our office manager, Dr Josefovits. It concerned a rather delicate matter. He was entrusted with the sum of no less than 870,000 *pengö* (even at that time a very considerable amount of money) belonging to Raoul Wallenberg, who had disappeared from Budapest two months earlier, and which had been left with Berg by Wallenberg's secretariat. A smaller amount, 100,000 *pengö*, could be retained by the Red Cross in settlement of the provision granted us by our Central Committee in Stockholm the year before. The remainder was to be exchanged for hard currency at the highest possible rate and brought by us to Bucharest for further transport via Berg to Wallenberg's title-holder in Stockholm. The plan was not badly conceived, and if it had succeeded might well have benefited any further relief work on the part of the Swedish organisation. In fact, however, the matter took quite a different course, as will be recounted later.

First on the bill, however, were the deposits in the embassy safe. At the time of the embassy staff's visit to our house, there were a few ladies living with us who had gone through hard times on the Buda side of the river, even in the relatively sheltered circumstances that the embassy premises offered. Apart from Berg's two secretaries – who were now alone at the embassy following his departure – and a couple of women from our own circle of acquaintances, there were two foreign women of a rather singular type.

One of them, a Greek countess by the name of Vlachos, reportedly related to our own royal family, is said to have spent months as the guest of the ambassador, and now claimed to have been given the task of blowing open the safe we have been talking about. All of these circumstances gave us little reason to doubt her word. The second lady in question, the wife of an Italian embassy secretary, Count Ferraris, who had remained loyal to the Italian king and had been captured by the Germans, had similarly claimed extraterritorial protection for a number of months, but through her bumptious mannerisms was beginning to get on the staff's nerves. I finally had to promise to secure a suitable hiding place for her during the Arrow Cross period. After a great deal of trouble and at risk of being discovered, one dark evening I gathered together her two little girls and the many items of luggage they had concealed in different places, and conveyed them to a safe haven in one of our convents. Ever dissatisfied with whatever was being done for her, she moved from there after a time and passed out of my knowledge. Some time during the devastating bombardment that took place at the beginning of the New Year it appears that the embassy either would not or could not refuse her refuge in their hopelessly overcrowded premises, and it was from there she now landed up among us. These two ladies entered into some kind of conspiracy with a certain Narich, who had previously been employed in the so-called B department, but who now through our mediation enjoyed the protection of the Italian community. This trio drew up a plan, in collaboration with some Yugoslav partisans who had mysteriously got hold of a lorry, to carry out the task of dynamiting and emptying the safe in question, at the same time recovering the ladies' personal effects which still remained at the embassy.

Our own involvement in all of this would merely be to receive the rescued deposits at our premises, well-guarded as they were against any looting. What to do with them subsequently would be a later question. As I had not yet recovered from my heavy cold, nor received any further assignment on behalf of the embassy, it was considered convenient to entrust the storage of the deposits to our loyal colleague Father J. Raile, head of the Papal Nuncio's social relief section, and very highly regarded by both our ambassador and my own friend, Archbishop Rotta, whose deputy in the Vatican's social relief organisation he had already been appointed.

On their return from the expedition to open the safe, versions of what had happened differed considerably, but the gist of the matter was the following: It had not been possible to blow open the safe, but instead the back had been opened up from a room behind using pick and crowbar. Its spacious interior contained a number of sealed packages each with a registration number; a trunk which was locked, but which later turned out to be the property of Sixten Bayer; a huge, antique silver chest, sealed under lock and key – a precious relic from the past deposited by the Teleki family; and finally a number of different objects of varying types. The silver chest together with some of the portable articles, which it was difficult to heave up on to the lorry, were stuffed into a sack and put in the trusting care of a loyal servant there – the excellent embassy head cook – to be stored in a safe (!) place. All the rest was thrown up on the lorry in great haste, just as a particularly nasty character was approaching from the top of the street, an individual there was every reason to fear.

It was the embassy . . . chauffeur! Of Slovakian descent, this
fellow had earlier had to replace the skilful mechanic employed
by our former ambassador Undén, and who had had to retire
from his job – albeit with a pension – and who, owing to his
Jewish background, had been called up for compulsory long-
term military service. After finally being released, he was
employed by me for Red Cross work, which he performed
exceedingly well. Later on we were instrumental in preventing
him and his family from falling into the clutches of the
deportation hounds, and he made it to safety in Switzerland,
although not before undergoing a six-month so-called 'cure' in
the (and now we know all about the place) oh so charming
Bergen-Belsen! While working for the Red Cross this man was
hated and persecuted by the embassy chauffeur, who tried to
betray him to the Germans, luckily without success. Our
Slovak, it must be said, enjoyed a reputation among the
embassy staff of being impudent, unreliable, lazy and a bit of
a thief. At the same time, however, he was crafty and intelligent
enough to make good use of his position and a certain
confidence his boss had in him to extort certain favours, as far
as obtaining a regular Swedish passport, albeit with a limited
period of validity. It is only to be hoped that he never manages
to get it extended by some innocent embassy official in another
country . . .

Heartily loathed by one and all, during the latter part of his
service with us this man was seen to be little more than a
downright scoundrel, prepared to commit any amount of
misdemeanours, sheltering under the cloak of a bigoted
Catholic. There is no doubt that during the various regimes
which held power in 1944–5 he trimmed his sails according to
the wind and offered his services as a spy to different masters,
betraying the provider of his bread-and-butter to Germans, the
Arrow Cross and marauding gangs, according to how it served
his interests best. As nobody else up there at the embassy could
understand Russian, our Slovak with his Slavic tongue was
able to pass himself off as an interpreter and wheedle his way
into such jobs at the first opportunity. As soon as all the

embassy officials had left the building following the order to leave the country, he made himself cock of the walk by exercising a reign of terror among the remaining staff by virtue of his supposed 'connections'. He appears to have carted off whole loads of stolen goods, partly on his own, and partly with the aid of his various henchmen, without any significant intervention taking place, probably as a result of bribing one or other of the members of the staff.

This, then, was the individual who now appeared on the scene. He had with him a Russian soldier who he ordered to inspect the lorry.

'Have you opened the safe?' he asked in an authoritative manner.

'No, we have just fetched Mme Ferraris' many trunks and miscellaneous belongings.'

'Good, because I have orders from the authorities to take charge of the safe,' he lied to them. Whereupon he dismissed the soldier and allowed our party, scared stiff as they were, to scuttle away, with their own 'loot' rescued.

This is how this adventurous expedition came to a happy end. We took charge of the deposits, listing them and locking them away; twenty or so packages in all, each with a registration number. A list of all of these deposits must have existed somewhere, but it was not found in the safe and has never been found since, to the best of my knowledge.

Since we neither found it advisable nor had the opportunity to drag these packages with us to Sweden, after a careful check of each individual case they were gradually handed over to their respective owners, with the exception of four. These bore a Swedish address, clearly indicated, and in the course of time they were delivered to Ambassador Danielsson for further transport. If the recipients' joy back home had only been a fraction of that shown by the Hungarians who recovered their precious articles on the spot, so to speak, then we could have felt really happy, although to tell the truth it should be added that often little gratitude was expressed, at least on the surface. A case in point I remember was that of a higher ministry official – an 'Aryan', to be sure! – who had wept and cursed his luck for as long as he was convinced his valuables had been lost (though both he and his mother had our letters of protection to thank for their survival), but who now grabbed his precious package and raced off as fast as his legs would carry him, never to be seen again.

Countess Ferraris, however, created a scandalous commotion, complaining that 'the Swedes had stolen the five jewel cases she had entrusted to storage' (which she evidently hoped to find in the safe) and had only left the forty-two chests piled up on the lorry. In the haste and general confusion which we were unable to do anything about, she took the trunk which belonged to Sixten Bayer. When he at last was informed that the safe had been broken open and had got his trunk back, it was found to have been opened and everything of value removed: mostly family jewels and high-value currency in cash, including some 8,000 Swiss francs. All that remained were a summer suit and an old dress. So far it appears that no explanation has been forthcoming of how this came about. If Bayer had at least been called to be present at the dynamiting of the safe, he would have been able to recover his belongings himself and these unfortunate events and suspicions would have been avoided.

Following the departure of the embassy staff our activities became in reality twofold: partly that of continuing our general relief work to the extent that our means and resources allowed pending reinforcement from home, and partly the job of acting, as it were, as administrator of the Swedish estate since no steps had been taken for this eventuality. It included care of the embassy building and any Swedish property remaining there plus emergency aid to members of the Swedish and other Scandinavian communities.

As far as the first matter was concerned, we could count on active engagement from both authorities and various special organisations working towards the same ends as ourselves. A matter of considerable importance, of course, was co-ordinating the work of these organisations so as to share out tasks in a sensible and friction-free manner. For this purpose a committee was formed of representatives of the municipal authorities in Budapest, the national Community Aid organisation and the Papal Nuncio together with the International, Hungarian and Swedish Red Cross units. The delegate from the last-named was unanimously elected chairman in recognition of the energetic and fruitful work we had been carrying out ever since the middle of the previous year. Meetings were held weekly at premises set aside by the city for our benefit; any steps and measures taken were recorded in a report, and the various tasks involved in the relief work were shared out accordingly so that effort and resources could be applied at those points where need was greatest.

As the city gradually took over health care, we were accordingly able to confine that part of our activity to providing medicine and drugs, of which we still had a reasonable supply. The soup kitchens we maintained were those in our immediate or close vicinity, especially since poor transport facilities prevented us from going further afield. Our own Red Cross kitchen fed as many people as space permitted, and from our stores we supplied food to visiting Scandinavians as well as a number of other needy people. This included above all mothers with small children and the elderly who needed to supplement the meagre nutrition they were able to obtain by their own efforts. I'll never forget the touching beam of happiness shown by a high-ranking old gentleman on receiving a few bottles of tomato purée and some home-baked buns from our kitchen to liven up his exceedingly sparse diet.

Otherwise it was mostly peas, beans, potatoes, carrots and other vegetables we dealt out, and which made up our own daily diet. Now and again we could add some lard and a few expensively-acquired eggs. The fact that we were able to get hold of these items at all from a place far out in the countryside we owed to the existence of the ancient lorry referred to earlier, which was in such a battered and worn-out condition that no army unit would even consider requisitioning it!

The orphanages we had been running were also provided

with food, meagre though the supply was. We were unfortunately unable to obtain any large quantities from the places out in the country where they could be purchased. This was because in the first place we only had the poor old lorry, but also because we never received any financial assistance from Sweden to cover the costs of relief work in a foreign land. What we did have access to was a modest amount of the money remaining from income accrued in Hungary the year before, both in cash and from commodities. This we had been able to salvage owing to the outstandingly sturdy construction of our safe. Little or no financial support was to be expected from local people as most of our wealthy friends had lost nearly all they had owned.

On the contrary – we began to get into troubled waters when claims were made by orphanages not under our administration. Almost daily a call would come in from one or more of these orphanages requesting the payment of invoices dating from the beginning of December, which was the last time they had been reimbursed for children we had placed with them. The rate of remuneration had been fixed at 10 *pengö* per child per day, which would work out at some 300,000 *pengö* for the month of December alone, taking into account some fifty orphanages. Further fees for the following months had to be added, however, as the contracts had not been officially terminated and were therefore still in force. In brief, meeting these claims was more than our entire property was worth, even if we used up every last penny for this purpose.

When I pointed out that our ambassador had split off our operations concerning orphanages from the rest of our activities in the autumn, and that *our* Red Cross had no obligation to pay any orphanage debts, we were met with scepticism and ridicule. Were we trying to make out that there were *two* Swedish Red Cross organisations in Budapest?! If we chose to refuse to pay what the Swedish Red Cross had pledged itself to pay we would find ourselves faced with legal action, and we would doubtless end up having to assume full responsibility. There were, moreover, newspapers nowadays capable of informing the general public how the Swedes sneaked out of their clear obligations!

Thus what had happened was just what I had warned might happen: the existence of *two* Swedish Red Crosses in Budapest was something no Hungarian could be persuaded to understand, while the embassy's decision in November to split the organisation into two would lead to an extremely unpleasant situation. There was nothing for it but to promise payment up until the end of March, and assure the orphanages that if they only exercised a modicum of patience, they would see that Sweden did not baulk at its obligations. How and from where we could obtain the necessary money was a mystery, but the mystery *had* to be solved to avoid the name of Sweden being eternally associated with shame and ignominy.

Owing to the fact that direct communications with Sweden had not yet been secured, the only path left open to us was via Bucharest, where I had established contact by means of provisional private couriers. Ambassador Reuterswärd there, always sympathetic to a genuine problem, was approached by letter in which I explained our situation. Two possible solutions presented themselves: either we could request the necessary financial support from the Central Committee in Stockholm, or else we could have some of the money deposited by Berg with our office manager placed at our disposal. We were also able to report that we were visited almost daily by people who in tears and desperation complained they had lost the precious possessions they had deposited at our embassy and now stood at poverty's door. There were also people demanding the payment of bills the authenticity of which we had no means of checking, and which we would therefore be wise not to pay.

This report fortunately got to Bucharest before our embassy people left. It appears to have caused them widespread dissatisfaction, and it seems there was little understanding for the fact that there was no choice but to pay up if Sweden's good name was to be preserved. The censure, nevertheless, had to be borne with equanimity: the main thing was that the courier on his return brought authorisation to pay the outstanding debts using the Wallenberg funds. That problem, at least, was out of the way. Our Father Raile demanded all the invoices back, meticulously checked each item, and paid out close to 600,000 *pengö* in all for a verified specification of the number of children per day at each orphanage. A settlement was reached for each and every orphanage, and the entire unpleasant business was cleared up. Sweden's reputation was salvaged thanks to the Wallenberg supplement, to the everlasting honour of his already highly-esteemed name in accursed Hungary, where it is reported that his deeds are to be remembered by a street named after him and a statue to be raised in Szent István Square.

One drawback resulting from this was that the setting up of our own orphanages was delayed for the entire month Father Raile was checking and paying off the debts. One debt amongst all of these was definitely *not* going to be acknowledged. A certain Ms Pogány, previously employed as a voluntary worker, turned up one day at the embassy presenting a document which showed that she had been appointed by Asta Nilsson as her deputy. On the basis of this it was requested that we take over a contract with a hospital supplying it with maintenance equipment, a demand it was impossible for us to meet with the limited means at our disposal.

Once again it became clear how the policy of establishing *two* Red Cross organisations in the same city had been a grave mistake! Ms Pogány required us to post a letter to Stockholm stating that money be set aside solely for her use in order for her to carry on the work under her own steam. The final wording of the letter I do not know after it had been slightly modified.

This same Ms Pogány, whose energy, willingness to work and love of Sweden deserve every praise, turned out to be one of those with written authority to look after and protect certain items of embassy property in the building. This included collecting some of the movable property, such as the better-quality carpeting and various utensils, to which she gave a secure home in a convent nearby where they would remain under lock and key until such time as a Swedish embassy was reinstated in Budapest and the items returned. The historic silver chest belonging to the Teleki family was among these items. When it was opened by its owners – its seal unbroken – the precious jewels it should have contained were found to be missing, however. Where, when and how they were removed remains to this day a complete mystery. Equally, a deposit placed in the same safe by Ms Pogány herself was missing, as well as another of inestimable value belonging to the Norwegian-born Edla Hubay, who claimed to have lost all she owned in the way of jewellery and precious stones.

One of the worrisome duties that fell to our lot following the embassy's departure was seeing to the well-being of members of the Scandinavian community in Budapest, in addition to restoring the embassy – if possible – to a habitable state. Without any authorisation to begin with, there was little I could do other than obtain police protection by approaching the prime minister's office. I had the ambassador's grand piano, damaged by rain and sun, brought in from the garden where it had been dumped, and had new locks fitted on all the doors. Before these security measures could be carried out, however, the grand piano was removed from the building once again, this time for good, by a gang of marauders, who carted it off to an unknown destination!

As far as the members of the Scandinavian community were concerned, we did receive some much appreciated help from Bucharest. Food was purchased with money placed at Bucharest's disposal by the Swedish Foreign Office, and was dispatched to us by lorry for distribution to the needy through the mediation of the International Red Cross. These lorryloads arrived at irregular intervals, however, and costs were quite high, with the result that it was decided to remit money instead in small amounts using reliable couriers. The need was urgent in some cases. Ms Hubay, for instance, previously owned a considerable fortune which included a large country estate and three houses with a very valuable art collection which had been totally destroyed, and she was reduced to little more than the clothes she stood up in. Pending the arrival of the Swedish money, we were limited to granting an advance from the Red Cross cash fund in the hope that the state would cover this outlay, which it appears to have done. In order to relieve our workload, the distribution process was entrusted to two capable members of the office staff of the Swedish Match Company, previously one of our clients and now willing to help out in this fresh task.

We were in desperate need of medical supplies and, for this purpose, I had already in February, on my visit to the government in Debrecen and instructed by the Foreign Minister, made representations to the Swedish government for their delivery by air. At the end of six weeks a telegram sent on 16 March informed us that an aircraft loaded with medical supplies would be despatched on two special conditions. Unfortunately the wording was difficult to decipher, so that neither the Hungarian Foreign Ministry – which had now moved over to the Pest side of the river – nor we ourselves were properly able to interpret the first of the conditions. The second condition involved obtaining landing permission from the Russian authorities. I was asked to approach the Soviet control commission in this matter and did my best, but was unsuccessful despite having to trudge on foot through a city still without any transport at all. The only solution, it seemed, was to telegraph Sweden requesting landing permission via diplomatic links between Stockholm and Moscow. And that's where the matter ended up. The transport had not arrived by the time of my departure in May, and in all probability up to the present day still has not been given the go-ahead.

The day of our departure from Budapest was approaching. Our embassy people had left Bucharest on 3 and 4 April for Stockholm via Odessa and Moscow. At about the same time the Papal Nuncio, Archbishop Rotta, and his Italian suite were transferred by train from Budapest to Istanbul. As far as we were concerned, the Control Commission had informed us that as a member of the Swedish embassy I would have to leave the country but could for the moment continue my work with the Red Cross, and would be welcomed back as soon as Sweden had recognised the new government – there was no immediate hurry as it was intended to make evacuation trains available in both May and June. I would be able to take with me whatever I wanted – documents, paperwork, valuables (of these all we now owned were our wedding rings!) – but no furniture. Everything would be properly sealed without inspection and sent along with us free of charge all the way via Moscow to Stockholm. The conditions under which we were to travel were, then, very favourable; after reporting that the packing had been completed and that my health was satisfactory, I would be given a definite date of departure.

The job now was to arrange for the continuation of Red Cross work during my temporary absence. Here it was that our excellent relations with the Hungarian authorities stood us in good stead. A man at the top who we managed to engage for our organisation was none other than the president of the National Assembly, Professor Zsedényi, who had also transferred his offices to the capital – to the parliament building which had escaped serious damage in the fighting. Directly under him as chairman was the former president of the National Bank, the country's leading financial institution, Dr Leopold Baranyai, a man who was also well-known in similar circles in Sweden. When the occasion required it, he had opposed the Germans' demand for a billion *pengő* credit in Hungary and had therefore been forced to resign. At the time of the March 1944 *coup d'état* he was taken prisoner and held under close arrest for four months, until the change of government in the summer.

Father Jacob Raile was elected as my personal deputy on our Red Cross committee, a post which also involved heading our child care department. In addition he headed the Papal Nuncio's social service section, which had been provided with ample space to work in within our building, and he had for a long time been one of our very best collaborators: as the leading figure at a Jesuit monastery nearby he had saved the lives of a number of people, including that of our engineer Forgó, whom it will be remembered was refused Swedish citizenship. In his capacity as administrator of his Order's property in the city and real estate in the countryside, he possessed considerable financial know-how, together with a knack of operating which enabled him to set up a whole range of orphanages as far as our own economic means would stretch.

In tandem with the powerful Catholic Church, the Protestant churches were represented on our committee by Dean (now Bishop) Lajos Wolf-Ordas, whose attempt to establish a common church initiative has been described earlier. The vital interests of the health care sector were looked after by one of our most loyal collaborators in the medical profession, Sándor Fekete. He was head of the Apponyi foundation's highly esteemed out-patient department, a model of medical administration. Side by side with him worked Reszö Oberländer, the head of a couple of the country's largest pharmaceutical companies.

We were assured of direct contact with the government through another member of our committee, Under-secretary of the Treasury István Vásárhely, who in his capacity as the minister's closest colleague was in charge of no less than four sections in the government administration. During the brief Arrow Cross period he was forced to go into hiding, though he nevertheless found the opportunity to work at my secretariat, much to our mutual benefit.

The last, but in all truth, the most important person I wish to name in this particularly notable group of personalities was our indefatigable office manager and 'general secretary', the lawyer László Josefovits, a member of the so-called 'people's court' who had been appointed city councillor by the middle-class party organisation. He had been with us almost right from the start, had shared our every risk and hazard, had been hunted down by his enemies as if he were their quarry, a wild animal out in the forest, and following the founding of the new republic was the very first to put his mind to the work that had to be done. A man rich in ideas, enjoying the best connections, he had an amazing capacity for work and a crafty way of overcoming every obstacle. His close connections included the chairman of the political party he supported, who after the coming elections would probably enter the ministry as its head. One example of his cunning was how during a visit to Debrecen he managed to conjure up enough foodstuffs for us to satisfy every need for a long time into the future. He was also the one whose brilliant idea was to found a Swedish–Hungarian Society in Budapest – *Svéd–Magyar Társaság* – which would come to be of vital importance as events developed during the final act of our Swedish drama.

As March came to an end the Russian guard we had benefited from almost from the start of the year was considered to be unnecessary and was withdrawn. Things nowadays were quite calm and normal in the city, but to make doubly sure a normal police patrol was posted outside our building. The government had long ago been reinstalled in the capital, while the municipal authorities similarly had resumed their usual duties. The streets had been cleared of the worst of the debris, a number of tramlines were once again in working order, the papers were back on the newsstands, shops, restaurants and cafés were opening up here and there, and most goods were on sale again, though generally at a price a hundred times what we had been used to. Only house rents had been stabilised – thus what I was paying a month for a partially-looted four-room flat was equivalent to the price of half a pound of butter or 150 grams of sugar! You'd have to pay close to 10,000 *pengö* for a tailored suit and 2,000 for a decent pair of shoes. I once was given a litre of milk as a present, said to have cost no more than 50 *pengö*. Out in the countryside these items could be bought for less, though generally not for money – payment was often made by offering clothes you were no longer wearing (inasmuch as you still had any!), which was seldom the case as most people had no more than what they stood up in. In spite of everything, however, life went on and began to slip back into the familiar, age-old channels.

Before our 'green berets' withdrew, they did us a final, much appreciated service. Our undamaged safe, which we could not open as the key to it had been deposited with the embassy and lost, and which we could not take with us owing to its enormous weight and the lack of transport, was cracked open with a sledge-hammer by one of the stout Russian soldiers belonging to our guard unit, enabling us to retrieve the valuable items inside and take them home with us. When offered a reward for this noble good deed, the soldier said he would be happy with a packet of cigarettes. We naturally added a small sum of money, but this Russian boy's pretensions stood in glaring contrast to what Narich's Yugoslav party fellows are said to have demanded for a similar service performed at the embassy building: half a million *pengö*! Narich, who maintained he had already paid this amount to the partisans, demanded that we reserve a similar amount on a pro-rata basis from the deposited contents of the safe. We naturally rejected this proposal as utterly unreasonable and unjustifiable, if not quite simply impossible to carry out, whereupon he had the cheek to suggest breaking into the Romanian embassy's safety deposit box and withdrawing the sum of money in question! Such a procedure was of course even more unthinkable – how he finally resolved his dilemma was his own business, for we had no desire to have a finger in that pie!

It was now April, and schools and universities were to open after Easter Week, to the extent, that is, that classes could be held in rooms and lecture halls rendered windowless. I dutifully registered my willingness to resume my teaching as lecturer at the university, and students would doubtless turn up in surprisingly large numbers. The faculty reported, however, that only a tiny number of classrooms could be put into shape for the most essential university subjects, and the Swedish language certainly wasn't one of them. On the other hand, I was very welcome back the following term when it was hoped things would have been more or less restored to normal conditions. Popping in to have a look at my classroom I found on one of the desks a significant 'relic' of what had been happening in the last few months: an abandoned ten-cartridge case of steel-jacketed machine-gun bullets! The Germanic languages department library resembled the baleful destruction of Jerusalem, and I was as pleased as Punch at my earlier decision not to have left our small Swedish library there but instead consigned it to a Jewish friend whose home was being protected by signs and plaques indicating it was a Swedish study circle centre, a tactic which was amazingly successful. Similarly, over a longer period of time the well-known pianist Annie Fischer's mother was protected by me 'leasing out' her flat, according to the notices we fixed to the door, advertising the place as a Scandinavian literary agency, with me as proprietor of the 'firm'. I should by rights have continued along the same path and established a music shop and book publisher, etc., but there's a limit to one's time!

As I was saying, at the start of April the Papal Nuncio had left, and we could have gone along too, though we wouldn't have been able to join our embassy people, who had just left Bucharest. A few days after they had reached Stockholm, the news of which we picked up on the radio and later read about in the press, a telegram was sent – on 23 April – from the Foreign Office to Bucharest ordering the Langlets to make their way home to Sweden immediately, indicating that 'Swedish Red Cross activity in the absence of a Swedish embassy is not permitted'.

This final decision did not reach us until the beginning of May when Ambassador Reutersward in Bucharest managed to get a copy over to us in Budapest by private courier. My response took the same route, emphasising the fact that our departure was fully dependent on the decision of the Russian Control Commission as there was no possibility of making an independent departure. As for the Red Cross, we had no other option but to follow orders and shut up shop. There was little or no reason for this when all the time that we had been operating there was a large section of the population in dire need of our help, and the activity was not only tolerated but seen as eminently desirable and urgently needed by the Hungarian authorities.

Discontinuing the relief work would have been sheer madness, not to say criminal, and as fortune would have it such a step did not have to be taken. The matter was resolved quite easily as follows: the same day the Red Cross closed its offices, its flag was removed and printed matter and sign-posting destroyed, the Swedish–Hungarian Society took its place with the same management, staff, premises and sphere of operations as its predecessor. We were now, in other words, a *Hungarian* organisation, independent of Sweden, and I was in a position to hand over all our property with a clear conscience as not a penny of financial assistance had come from our home country. All we owned had been in the shape of gifts from Hungarian sources personally placed in our hands. On arrival back in Sweden I had every reason to claim that hardly ever had Swedish Red Cross relief work abroad on such a scale been performed without the slightest sacrifice on the part of the Central Committee.

The Swedish–Hungarian Society had, of course, a much wider programme of activities than just social welfare. It consisted basically of three branches of work. One of its departments was concerned with information of a commercial nature in the absence of a Swedish embassy and in want of a Swedish–Hungarian chamber of commerce. No business between Sweden and Hungary had taken place since the trade agreement had ceased to be in force a year previously, nor could it feasibly be expected within the foreseeable future. Nothing stood in the way of building a little, however small, for the future, and a few salvaged manuals with details of companies, their addresses, etc., might be of some service to a reborn Hungarian business community. To lead this department we succeeded in extracting a promise from a particularly vigorous source: Franz Pirkner, for many years head of the world-renowned Swedish Ball Bearing Company's subsidiary in Hungary.

Another department at the Society dealt with cultural affairs, and was able to base its efforts on the exceptional goodwill created in the country by the Swedish Days exhibition held in Budapest in 1943. Its initial phase would have to be confined to some preparatory work, but in the future its activities could have great significance in forging cultural links between our two countries. Our proposal as far as head of this section was concerned was an all-rounder in the person of a former departmental head in the Hungarian education and culture ministry, who had been stripped of everything he possessed by the Arrow Cross, but who now willingly made himself available for the post.

The third branch of activity – and under the circumstances the most important of all – concerned a social programme of relief work. It was put in the hands of our former Red Cross committee, the excellent composition of which – referred to previously – was a guarantee of the greatest possible efficiency. Its honorary chairman, President of the National Assembly Zsedényi, immediately assured us he was prepared to take up a similar post in the new organisation. This gave us a fully guaranteed unbroken link between government, parliament and political parties. We could count on the favourable disposition of the competent authorities since the committee included a number of important government officials. Members of the government expressed their very sincere regret at my departure, but were equally happy that operations nonetheless could continue. The Prime Minister himself expressed the keen hope in seeing me again soon, and I responded assuring him that nobody would be happier than I, should fate design it so.

In expectation that following my return to the land of my birth – set for sometime in June – relief supplies could finally be sent from Sweden in respectable proportions (above all from firms which had previously had good business experiences with Hungary and would probably wish to restore trade), our optimism knew no bounds and we went ahead and proceeded to expand our field of work.

As early as in April we had, in co-operation with other organisations, opened an important branch of work taking care of the swarms of deportees from the liberated areas of Germany who were returning having survived the slavery they had been subjected to. We now wished to lighten the burden of these troubled individuals. Most of the people we were helping did not own more than one set of clothes, and needed assistance in getting them mended or exchanged. For this purpose we intended setting up sewing and needlework centres where they would be able to seek help. Working mothers – and what mother did not now have to go out and earn her daily bread! – needed crèches and kindergartens for their children while they were at work. New orphanages were in demand, and it was Father Raile's big responsibility to get these started on the Nuncio's account as well as the Society's.

Aid in the shape of money and commodities from countries which could afford to be generous was needed for all of this, and is still needed, especially for the winter months. We reckoned, and are still reckoning, on aid from prosperous Sweden in the first place. This has been forthcoming through the energetic and successful work carried out by the Save the Children Fund. Nevertheless, there is a hungry and freezing population suffering daily, young and old alike, and they deserve our immediate care and attention. A helping hand should therefore be offered to *all* in need, as far as we in our fortunate land, spared these hardships, are able to give of ourselves. We can't come to the aid of everybody, but with a little goodwill it's within our power to perform charitable acts which will be an abiding memory of Swedish humanitarianism and love for one's neighbour.

Apart from all of this our organisation was faced with a practical problem it would have been folly to ignore. Besides the evacuation of embassy staff from neutral countries who still remained in Budapest, the Russian Control Commission wanted to invite all foreign nationals to consider returning to their native countries. They therefore requested of us that we arrange for the documents of Swedes, Danes, Norwegians and even Finns applying to leave the country to be examined, instructing them on how such a possible return trip home should proceed. We were obliged to attend to a daily flow of

applicants which often put considerable demands on our
capacity, all the more so as a number of hesitant persons who
could not make up their minds whether to leave or not kept
turning up at our door to ask for advice. It was a rather delicate
job we had on our hands and far from easy to tackle, especially
when it concerned women who had married Hungarians and
were no longer citizens of a Scandinavian country. Another
difficulty loomed in the shape of the many holders of
provisional passports which had expired, and who, according
to the instructions we had received, would not be able to count
on these passports being extended. While I was performing
this work as a kind of voluntary consultant – not to say consul
without official status – I otherwise used my time, pending the
arrival of the evacuation train, in helping put the embassy
building in some sort of habitable shape. Joining Pirkner, who
I knew enjoyed the full confidence of the embassy, we carried
out a thorough inspection of the building. A heavy bomb was
discovered to have opened up a huge crater in the garden. Rain
and snow had spread from there into an air-raid shelter nearby,
and a nauseous stench pervaded the whole area. The stagnant
water had to be pumped out while the crater was filled in with
boulders and earth. The roof of the embassy building had been
badly damaged, and it was absolutely vital to get it fixed to
prevent rain seeping through and damaging an interior that
was otherwise in fairly good condition. Sixten von Bayer took
upon himself this responsibility in his capacity as representative of the proprietors of the building, who incidentally
were set back quite a tidy sum with this repair. Shell damage
to a couple of the balconies could be seen to, in our view, at a
later date, but all the shattered window panes needed immediate attention. Ceilings, walls and floors were in good shape and
required no restoration. Equally, furnishings and paintings,
etc., the property of the Swedish state, merely needed
rearranging and a freshening-up. Through my intervention a
former member of the domestic staff, who had also acted as
concierge in a neighbouring building, had sorted out and
tidied up a mass of books and papers which lay strewn around.

With his customary zeal and fervour Pirkner promised to clear up whatever remained to be done. The costs to be borne would unfortunately have to come out of any surplus in the amount of money deposited by Berg, after the orphanage debts had been settled. My intention was, immediately on arrival home in the middle of June, to procure payment to cover this outlay. Victor Langhard, our expert in agricultural matters and a senior member of the Swedish community who had been living for months with us at the Red Cross building, was urged to move into the embassy together with his son and domestic staff to keep an eye on the work being carried out and take care of state property, until such time as the foreign office had made other arrangements. As the entire embassy domestic staff had removed itself to an unknown destination, Bayer employed an entirely new and reliable concierge. A comprehensive report was drafted of all the measures that had been taken, and would be sent to the competent authorities in Sweden as soon as a suitable occasion arose.

There was one more area where I took certain liberties, prepared as I was to face any possible disapproval in good spirits. Some of our friends expressed the wish to preserve the memory in some permanent fashion of the Swedish Red Cross achievements in Hungary during the dramatic period of 1944 and 1945. We then came to an agreement that the best form for this would be to connect its name to some hospital, or at least some hospital ward or department. A number of hospitals in the city had suffered varying degrees of damage during the fighting. If we could put one of these into functional use, perhaps this could present an opportunity. By chance, very close to us was a smallish hospital attached to the university essentially reserved for academic members of the citizenry. The building had been damaged but could be repaired at a reasonable cost. The necessary equipment was available, both surgical and medical, but there was a lack of funds to make the building fully functional.

The university vice-chancellor – as such, of course, my own superior – happened to be an eminent physician, Professor

Frigyesi, with whom we had earlier had a good deal of very fruitful collaboration. He was very worried over the fact that the hospital lay empty, and enormously grateful that we were in a position to offer him assistance in getting it operating again. It would be a never-to-be-forgotten helping hand, and he made a commitment to give the hospital the name *Svéd Vörös Kereszt Egyetemi Kórház*, meaning the Swedish Red Cross Academic Hospital, reserving a certain number of beds in the first place for members of the Swedish community in Budapest.

A team of experts was consulted to make a thorough inspection and estimate costs. They concluded that a very modest sum was needed for a complete overhaul, to which minor additions might be made to cover costs for free treatment for fifty or so persons during the first year of operation or until the end of 1946. The university henceforth would be responsible for further costs, on the understanding that a sufficient number of paying patients made the activity financially viable. A contract was drawn up containing these conditions, and all that remained for me (!) was to secure the financial means. Providence smiled kindly on me that day as the very same afternoon a lady friend declared herself willing to make an immediate loan in Swiss francs to cover the costs of repairs. I hadn't the slightest doubt that once home in Sweden I could procure money for maintenance costs. Pirkner took charge of the business and agreed to oversee the financial administration on our account as superintendent, while the university would be appointing a head physician and would be responsible for patients' care and treatment.

A tender for the job was received from the head of the Apponyi out-patients department we referred to earlier. If all goes well, and if a 100,000 *kronor* grant can be secured from Sweden, the Swedish Red Cross will have its name perpetually linked to *two* institutions in Budapest, to the benefit primarily of Swedish residents there as well as many people in situations of acute distress. I have every reason to hope this will turn out successfully, if only my appeal reaches well-intentioned and open-hearted people in my home country.

While these negotiations with the hospital were going on, the Russian Control Commission had set the departure date for the evacuation train at May 26. All we had to do was make our dutiful farewells and pack the belongings we were still fortunate to have and wished to take with us. Among us on the evacuation train were people from other embassies who were *obliged* to leave Hungary, as well as foreigners who simply *wished* to leave and were in possession of sufficient documentation for entry into the countries they were going to.

The train consisted of a score or so of goods wagons lacking any facilities whatsoever. We fitted out the Swedish wagon with packing-cases and bedding so as to convert it into a quite acceptable 'wagon-lit', where by force of circumstances we would be spending all of ten days and nights.

The journey was quite an experience, and ended in an amazing fashion. Four hundred people of ten different nationalities were accommodated on the train: Swedes, Danes and Finns, who were then to travel north from Bucharest homewards, and Greeks, Italians, Swiss, French, Belgian and Dutch, who would be continuing their journey via Istanbul in a westerly direction by steamboat. In addition, there were a number of Hungarian Jews armed with entry permits to the respective country where they had close relatives living. Each wagon was decked with its national flag or colours, and on the journey came to be decorated with twigs, branches and flowers producing a festive appearance. We all had various items of food with us – to the extent that such could be obtained – and the food was cooked on a Primus stove or over a fire we lit between the bricks and stones of the railway embankment. Hygienic requirements and relieving ourselves meant seeking out the nearest bushes whenever we stopped during the journey. When a river or lake was passed and we stopped, the scene presented a motley crowd of bathers.

Travelling through the springtime Hungarian lowlands, a matter of a few hundred kilometres, took three whole days. Next came the lovely hilly landscape of Siebenbürgen, and one icy, sun-lit morning the train came to a stop in a mountain pass at an altitude of 1,000 metres in the Transylvanian Alps, with a stunning vista of snow-covered peaks. Our subsequent descent brought us past the exquisitely beautiful Sinaia, which I now gazed at half a century after my youthful wanderings in these parts of the country. In the evening we passed the notorious Ploesti with its oil derricks and endless lines of tanker wagons waiting to be filled. It wasn't until night had fallen that our train rolled into the Bucharest station, where we were heartily welcomed by the Swedish embassy staff, with Ambassador Reuterswärd at their head.

This is where our Scandinavian wagon was to be uncoupled for our further transport northwards. The Russian station master confirmed this arrangement, and we prepared ourselves for a few days' rest in the Romanian capital which I had not seen for fifty years.

Fate, however, had decided otherwise. Only half an hour had passed when orders arrived from the Control Commission there – evidently not in touch with its 'sister' institution in Budapest – that our wagon, too, was to continue the journey to Istanbul, from where we were to find our way home as best we could. Without money for the voyage, and loaded down with a mass of luggage – and we had been promised a safe and comfortable journey home through Russia! Now, however, we were faced with a long haul through Bulgaria and Turkey, followed by a lengthy voyage by sea aboard some Swedish vessel, if we were lucky, across the Mediterranean and the Atlantic Ocean. Fortunately, the very considerate people at the Swedish embassy in Bucharest had thought of everything. We were provided with a more than adequate supply of food of a satisfying variety, and a plentiful amount of money in Romanian *lei*, enabling us to feel fully confident for the remainder of the train journey south, while similarly the International Red Cross delegation in Bucharest looked after the other passengers on the train.

The rest of the journey doesn't really belong here. Suffice it to say that the 1,000 kilometres or so through three countries meant five days of camp life in what were really cattle trucks;

a ferry took us over the broad stretches of the Danube at Russe, followed by a snail's-pace crawl over the winding passes of the Balkan mountains down to the God-forsaken Bulgarian border town of Svilengrad. After passing the fine-looking Adrianople we changed to a Turkish passenger carriage with a sleeping car for us 'diplomats', and on the morning of 5 June we swept into Istanbul railway station. The enormous medieval city wall, the lofty proud mosques, the dark-blue Sea of Marmara, the Bosporus and the Golden Horn – all of these wonders which I had gazed upon the first time with the romantic eyes of youth, now lay before us in the golden shimmer of the morning sun.

At the station, Consulate Secretary Weman met us on behalf of the embassy and took care of our every need in an impeccable manner. It almost seemed as if an effort was being made to outdo the Bucharest colleagues in sheer kindness. The old Turkish capital retained some of its Oriental charm after Atatürk had scraped away some of the more picturesque aspects of times past leaving the traditional dirt still in place. A few weeks' stay passed as in a dream, with a variety of excursions arranged for us in the indescribably beautiful surroundings pending the arrival of a suitable vessel to ship us home. The days were brightened up through the exquisite hospitality offered us in the charming old embassy hotel, where our *chargé d'affaires* Carl-Henrik von Platen and general consul Gislow together with their amiable and talented staff – not to forget other members of the Swedish community – made every effort to make things pleasant for us while we were awaiting the hour of departure.

At the turn of the month the Swedish Orient Line's longed-for M/S *Vasaland* finally put into port, and first-class accommodation on board had been reserved for us: the same cabin the royal prince and princess had travelled in when they accompanied the ship on its maiden voyage to the east. A couple of weeks' wait preceded the loading of the cargo, and then the handsome ship sailed for Smyrna. A further two weeks, and we were out in the breathtaking Greek archipelago on our way to terribly devastated Malta, and then on to Spain and Portugal. Not until 24 August were the bows of our ship pointing towards Göteborg, over the choppy seas of the Atlantic and the North Sea, leaving behind us the delightful city of Lisbon, bathed in a heady sunlight. On 2 September the lighthouse at Vinga in the Göteborg estuary was sighted, and through the calm and sparkling waters of the archipelago we approached the splendid port of Göteborg, where a warm welcome had been prepared for us by Hungarian friends, grateful for our efforts in their behalf back in Budapest.